SHORT HIKES
IN THE BERKSHIRES

High on Mount Greylock.

SHORT BIKE RIDES IN THE BERKSHIRES

Lewis C. Cuyler

photograph by Christopher Gillooly

Old Chester Road
Chester, Connecticut 06412

This book is dedicated to my mother, Margery (Merrill) Cuyler, who grew up in Stockbridge. She introduced me to both bicycling and Berkshire County long before I had a notion to write about either.

Lewis C. Cuyler
January, 1979

Unless otherwise credited, the photographs are by the author.

Copyright © 1979 Lewis C. Cuyler
Library of Congress catalog number 79-50694
ISBN: 0-87106-028-0

Manufactured in the United States of America
All Rights Reserved
First Edition

Foreword

Berkshire County is particularly inviting for bicycle tourists because its geography and history have combined to produce an environment especially high in the special quality that springs from a rich mixture of scenery, culture and commerce.

This atmosphere is best experienced by bicyclists whose slower mode of transportation enables them to savor the county's sights, sounds and smells in a way unknown to travellers restricted by the confines of their automobiles.

The county has about 150,000 people who live in two cities, both of modest size, and 30 towns spread out over 947 square miles in a rectangular shape at the western end of Massachusetts. Bounded roughly by the Hoosac Mountain range on the east, the Taconic range on the west, dominated in the north by Mt. Greylock, the state's highest peak, and in the south by Mt. Everett, the county has always stood slightly apart from its neighbors. This is more of a matter of geography than the official boundaries that separate the Berkshires from the rest of Massachusetts and the neighboring states of Vermont, New York and Connecticut. Geography has shaped Berkshire history and bicyclists, as riders of machines that must constantly interact with the terrain, are particularly equipped to see the effects.

Because the county is hilly, Berkshire bicycling is definitely not for those who like their riding flat. In fact, none of the rides in the guide can be described this way. Rather, most of them are rolling, consisting of gradual uphills or downhills, with a few steep mountains in between.

The mountains, however, are not large enough to prevent good bicycling and roads follow the valleys in such a way that any bicyclist in good shape on a 10-speed machine will be rewarded by tours that are among the most scenic in New England, with many offering more points of interest per square mile than rides just about anywhere else in the country. Moreover, the county's many inns, motels and restaurants mean the rides can be taken in luxury, or, if budgets do not permit, in the cheaper accommodations of the conveniently spaced public campgrounds. Perhaps the best way to bicycle the county is to indulge in a little luxury tempered by the challenge of camping.

The county's modern history began in the 1700s when the first white settlers pushed over the Hoosac range to find the valleys carved from the mountains by the Housatonic River in the south and the two branches of the Hoosac River in the north. A century later the flow of the two major rivers and their tributaries were to supply water power for the huge textile mills that formed the economic underpinnings of the county's principal industrial communities: North Adams, Adams, Dalton, Pittsfield, Lee and Great Barrington.

But as industry began to take hold in the county, so did cultural attractions. In the 1800s, Berkshire County's outstanding scenery drew major writers in America to the area who were inspired to describe its beauty. Their work, along with growing industry, attracted people of great wealth, especially to the towns of Lenox, Stockbridge and Williamstown, who transformed the settings of these communities into parks with trees, luxurious lawns and wide streets, a heritage that remains today in the three towns.

Wealthy residents also established a climate of culture which in later years became Tanglewood in Lenox, the summer home of the Boston Symphony Orchestra; the Jacob's Pillow Dance Festival in Becket; the Williamstown Theatre Festival and the Sterling and Francine Clark Art Institute, both in Williamstown; the Berkshire Theater Festival in Stockbridge, and a host of art galleries and other cultural offerings.

For the bicyclist, who can sample the county's richness at a slower pace, this means a combination of trips that can be interspersed by visits to the theater and galleries, the experience of riding through mill towns, estate towns, and farm towns on challenging rides and easy rides, all at a pace and style of his or her own choosing.

The balance of this book is divided into seven chapters. The first contains information of general interest to the bicycle tourist. Chapter 2 describes the southwestern section that is marked by rolling country around Sheffield, Great

Barrington and West Stockbridge, and Chapter 3 tells about the estate towns of Lenox and Stockbridge as well as the industrial village of Housatonic.

Chapter 4 is about Pittsfield, the largest of the county's two cities and located in its very heart, and Chapter 5 describes trips up and over Mt. Greylock, the highest mountain in Massachusetts. Chapter 6 tells about rides in the northern part of the county where the mountains are steeper, the valleys narrower.

Finally, Chapter 7 attempts to put it all together by recommending an itinerary for a leisurely two-week trip through the county that incorporates the highlights of the previous rides.

As the prospective bicycle tourist will see, none of the individual rides takes more than a day, with the exception of the two-day trip over Mt. Greylock, and even that can be shortened to a day. Attempts have been made to make all of the trips loops, to route all of them on secondary roads with hard surfaces and still cover the major points of interest in the county. They do not cover all of the county and many places not mentioned make rewarding visits. For the purpose of this book, however, they were skipped either because the terrain was judged unsuitable or because the scenery was not varied enough. Care has been taken to make the distances mentioned accurate, but no two odometers ever seem to read the same, so the readings must be taken as approximations that at most are not too far off. To obtain the most benefit from this guide, you should equip your bicycle with an odometer.

As with any guidebook, the rides described represent only starting points. A careful study of a county map will show how they relate, how they can be varied or combined to accommodate a trip's needs. An exceptionally good map of Berkshire County is available from the county engineer's office in Pittsfield for $1.50.

Because of the hills, the Berkshire County rider should own, rent or borrow a properly fitted 10-speed bicycle equipped with a free wheel that has 28 or 32 teeth to provide a fairly low gear. The county has some bicycle shops, but riders should be prepared to perform their own repairs by bringing along a standard tool kit, tire patches and an air pump. The kit should also include a free wheel remover tool, a spoke wrench, an extra spoke or two, an adjustable crescent wrench to supplement the standard lightweight wrenches, tire irons and a small screwdriver. Other musts include a first aid kit, a water bottle and rear panniers and handlebar bags to carry the equipment. A backpack is not recommended for riding distances. Cameras go best in the handlebar bag where they are easily accessible.

I am indebted to Stephanie L. Johnson of The Transcript in North Adams and David Ennis, proprietor of the Pinnacle Bicycle Shop in Lenox, for helping me collect the information for this guide. By coincidence, Ms. Johnson was finishing a guide book to the Berkshires about the same time I was beginning mine. Her work, entitled "The Best of the Berkshires," describes her own choices of where to stay, where to buy, what to do and what to wear. I have read her guide in manuscript form and even though it is written primarily for the automobile tourist I highly recommend it as a supplement to this guide. In fact, with Ms. Johnson's permission I have borrowed from her research about sights to see.

A second important source has been a work entitled, aptly enough, "A Berkshire Sourcebook," a publication sponsored by The Junior League of Berkshire County and published in 1976. The author is William Carney and the illustrator Carol Hill.

While I hope there aren't any errors in this book, some are inevitable, given the size of the county. For these I am solely responsible and I apologize in advance for any inconvenience.

In closing, I hope that you enjoy reading about the trips as much as I have enjoyed writing about them. Better yet, I hope you can take them, and thus discover a Berkshire County you can never really see by car. In doing so, may I wish for the wind to be always at your back and for your hills to be always down, as the old greeting goes. I know too well that neither hills nor wind will always be the way you want them in Berkshire County, but nevertheless I am confident its other offerings will compensate.

LEWIS C. CUYLER
North Adams, Mass.
    January, 1979

Table of Contents

CHAPTER 1: **Getting Your Berkshire Bearings** 13

CHAPTER 2: **The Southwest Corner: Rambling and Rolling** 17
- Ride 1: Sheffield Swing-Around 17
- Ride 2: Great Barrington Short Loop 21
- Ride 3: Great Barrington Long Loop 24
- Ride 4: Great Barrington-North Egremont Loop 29
- Ride 5: Great Barrington-West Stockbridge Loop 32
- Ride 6: West Stockbridge-Pittsfield Loop 36

CHAPTER 3: **Estates and Industry: Stockbridge, Lenox and Housatonic** 41
- Ride 7: Stockbridge-Cherry Hill Challenge 47
- Ride 8: Stockbridge-Housatonic Loop 50
- Ride 9: Stockbridge-Lenox Loop 52
- Ride 10: Stockbridge Bowl Ride-Around 56
- Ride 11: Stockbridge-Chesterwood-Berkshire Garden Center 60
- Ride 12: Stockbridge-Lenox-South Lee-Tyringham-Monterey Workout............. 63

Ride 13: Lenox Landscaper 68
Ride 14: Lenox Lollipop 74
Ride 15: Lenox-Shaker Village ... 77
Ride 16: Lenox-Arrowhead-
Crane Museum and Stritch
Sculpture Gardens 82

CHAPTER 4: **Pittsfield: Berkshire's Urban Place** 87
Ride 17: Park Square to Dalton
and Hinsdale................... 88
Ride 18: Pittsfield Onota Lake
Ride-Around 93
Ride 19: North-South Link 96

CHAPTER 5: **Mount Greylock: Head for the Sky** 101
Rides 20A-E: Five Ways to the
Visitor's Center 102
Ride 21: Up and Over the "High
Lord of the Berkshires" 111

CHAPTER 6: **Northern Berkshire: Mount Greylock Surrounded** 115
Ride 22: Greylock Go-Around.... 118
Rides 23-23A: North Adams to
Cheshire to Adams Ramble...... 123
Ride 24: North Adams to
Williamstown and Back......... 128
Ride 25: Williamstown Short
Loop 132
Ride 26: Williamstown Longer
Loop 134
Ride 27: Figure 8 High-Low
from Williamstown to Hancock
to New Ashford and Back 137

CHAPTER 7: **Putting It All Together: Two Weeks on Berkshire Byways**...... 141

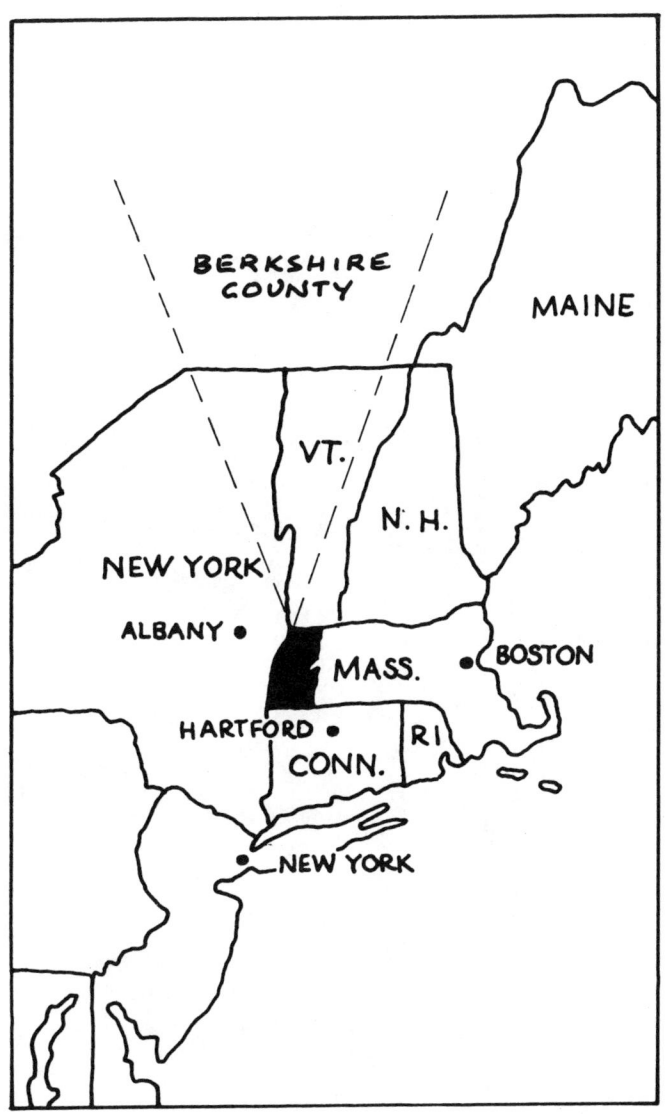

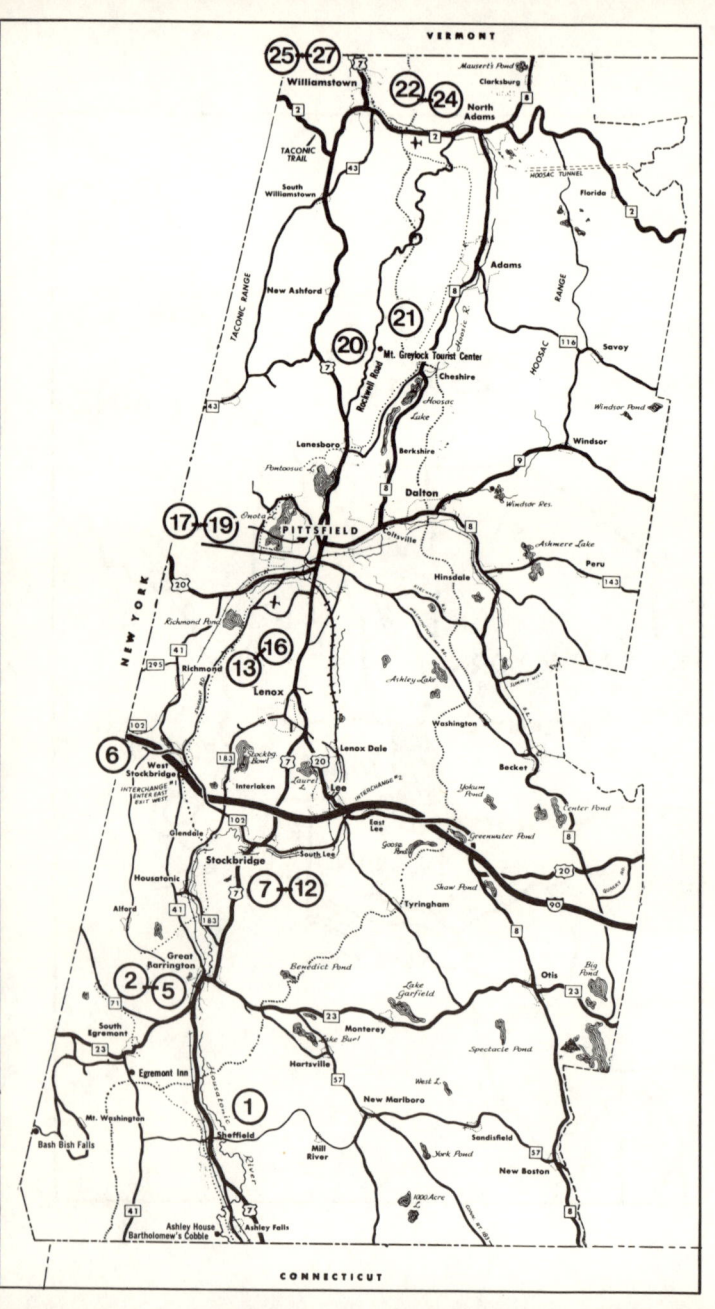

Chapter 1:
Getting Your Berkshire Bearings

Berkshire County is a large rectangle that occupies the entire far western end of Massachusetts, bordered on the north by Vermont, on the west by New York, on the south by Connecticut and on the east by an artificial line that runs roughly over a ridge of mountains and hills.

Depending on your destination, the county is a three to four hour drive from New York City, a three hour drive from Boston, about an hour's drive from Albany and two hours from Hartford, Connecticut.

Pittsfield has an airport served by Command Airways with flights daily from the New York City area, and charter service is also available from airports in Pittsfield, North Adams and Great Barrington. Bus service connects the county to New York, Boston, Albany, Hartford, New Haven and Burlington, Vermont.

If you are travelling by car, from New York take the Taconic Parkway. From Boston take the Massachusetts Turnpike to Lee, Pittsfield and West Stockbridge, or Route 2 to North Adams and Williamstown. From Connecticut, Route 7 will bring you to Sheffield, Great Barrington, Stockbridge, Lenox, Pittsfield and Williamstown, the start of most trips described in this guide.

Additional information about travel, reservations and what's happening may be obtained by telephoning or writing the county's tourist agency: Berkshire Hills Conference Inc., 20 Elm St., Pittsfield, Mass. 01201. The telephone is 413-443-9186.

Although the Berkshire Hills Conference is the best all around place to obtain information in advance of a trip, there are seven other information places in the county that bicyclists should know about. All have pamphlets, restaurant listings and summer schedules.

Their locations are:

Great Barrington: Chamber of Commerce booth at 362 Main St. (Route 7 opposite fairgrounds) open year-round;

Lee: On Route 20, corner of the park, open daily July and August, weekends only during fall;

Lee: Just off the Massachusetts Turnpike, at Howard Johnson's, open year-round;

Lenox: Chamber of Commerce booth open July and August in the Academy Building on Main Street;

North Adams: The Northern Berkshire Chamber of Commerce office, 69 Main St., open year-round, and at 1 Main St., Mohawk Center in summer only;

Stockbridge: On Main Street, open July and August;

Williamstown; Board of Trade booth at the corner of Main and North Streets (Route 2), open daily July and August, weekends through October.

Other information may be obtained from the two major daily newspapers serving the county, the *Berkshire Eagle* that circulates throughout the county, and *The Transcript,* which concentrates on north county. Both newspapers publish free summer magazines with listings of events and feature stories for the entire county. The Transcript's *SummerScope* is published bi-weekly in July and August and the Eagle's *Berkshire Week,* comes out weekly during the same months.

In addition, the Berkshire Vacation Bureau has three county numbers that can be called toll free for daily event listings. The numbers change yearly but are well publicized.

Camping

Camping is available at Beartown State Forest, Pittsfield State Forest, October Mountain State Forest, Clarksburg State Park, on Mt. Greylock and at other state areas less accessible to the rides described. North Adams has a municipal camping area and there are a number of private campgrounds whose names may be obtained from the tourist services. A list of state forests and parks, with additional information, is available by writing Massachusetts Department of Environmental Management, 100 Cambridge St., Boston, 02202, or its Region V office on Cascade Street, Pittsfield, Mass. 01201. The regional office telephone is 413-442-8928.

Bicycle Shops

At the time of writing, there were at least six bicycle shops in the county, four offering rentals, and all of them repairs and parts. They are Plaine's in North Adams and Pittsfield, The Spoke in Williamstown, Arcadian Shop in Lenox, Daly's in Pittsfield, Harland Foster Inc. in Great Barrington and Ron & Al's in Adams. The latter two do not offer rentals.

Hospitals

The county has four hospitals: North Adams Regional, Hillcrest and Berkshire Medical Center, both in Pittsfield; and Fairview Hospital in Great Barrington.

Chapter 2:
The Southwest Corner:
Rambling and Rolling

For the long distance bicyclist who likes rolling terrain, interesting vistas and roads with little traffic, the southwestern part of the county offers the best riding.

Rides 1 through 6 are distinguished by sweeping views of Mt. Everett or Monument Mountain, the largest peaks in south county, and all are marked by rolling farm land vistas, particularly on the roads nearest the county's western border between Sheffield and West Stockbridge.

Other parts of the county are less rural and have more historical and cultural offerings. But for sheer riding enjoyment, nowhere else in the county can beat the marvelous terrain of its southwestern section.

One of the cultural offerings in this section of the county is unusual in that its namesake had no direct connection with the county. The place is the Albert Schweitzer Friendship House and Library that is just west of Great Barrington and along the route of Rides 4 and 5. Mr. Schweitzer, who was one of the world's more celebrated humanitarians, so inspired filmmaker Erica Anderson that after his death in 1965 she established a museum and library to record his work. The center is considered to house one of the largest complete Schweitzer collections in the country.

Public camping and swimming in this section of the county can be found at the Beartown State Forest on Route 23, east of Great Barrington. It is accessible to Rides 1 through 5.

Ride 1: Sheffield Swing-Around
27.4 miles or, shorter version, 16.8 miles

The ride can begin either at Stagecoach Hill, one of New England's traditional country inns on Route 41, 4.8 miles from the center of Sheffield, or at the intersection of Route 7

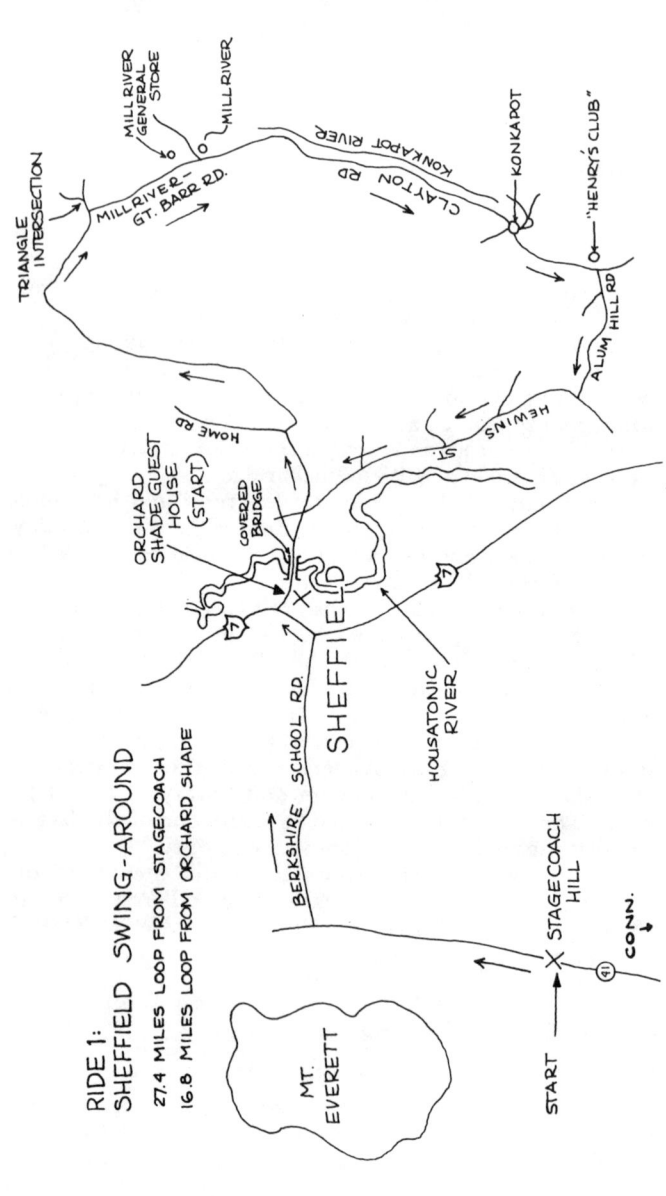

and County Road, just north of the town's center where riders can stay at the Orchard Shade, a lovely old New England home that has been a guest house since 1888. Stagecoach Hill offers full menu and cozy, intimate atmosphere, and the Orchard Shade offers bed and continental breakfast.

The ride, beginning at Stagecoach Hill, is 27.4 miles, and beginning at Orchard Shade (250 yards off Route 7) it covers 16.8 miles. Stagecoach Hill may be reached by taking Route 41 north from Salisbury, Connecticut, or Berkshire School Road west from Sheffield, then making a left and heading south for two miles on Route 41.

The route provides a good warm-up if you are planning to spend some time in the county, not only for muscles, but also for bicycles and the initial adjustments that must be made for most trips. The ride winds through back roads, some with bumpy surfaces, and features a covered bridge, a traditional New England general store in Mill River and magnificent views of 2,624 foot Mt. Everett that towers over southern Berkshire.

From Stagecoach Hill, head north on Route 41 for about two miles and then east on Berkshire School Road for 2.8 miles, through mostly flat country on roads with good surfaces. At Route 7, go left and head north for a half mile and then right on County Road where the sign points to New Marlboro. Almost immediately on your right is the Orchard Shade guest house, an alternative place for the ride's start.

Follow County Road east, going through a covered bridge, eight-tenths of a mile from Orchard Shade, and then start climbing a long, gradual hill until the intersection of County Road and the Mill River-Great Barrington Road, 5.7 miles from Route 7. The intersection is distinguished by a small woods-and-brush filled triangle with one arm going straight, the other bearing right. Bear right and head towards Mill River, a distance of 1.7 mostly downhill miles. You might want to consider a stop at the Mill River General Store for refreshment and local color.

At Mill River go right on Clayton Road, where the surface is bumpy for 4.0 miles to the right turnoff up over Alum Hill. On your left is the Konkapot River and about three miles along the road, at an intersection, is the center of Konkapot, which is not much more than a farm and a few buildings. Go for another mile, where you'll see "Henry's Club" on the left, and take the road opposite, a right turn, over Alum Hill for the steepest climb of the trip. At the top the first of many panoramic views of Mt. Everett appears. Go down the other side to the intersection of Hewins Street, a total distance of 1.4 miles from "Henry's", and make a right. Follow Hewins Street, a nice easy 3.1 mile meander with many views of Mt. Everett, back to County Road. Take a left, go through the covered bridge again and head towards Route 7 and completion of trip.

Summary: Ride 1

0.0   From Stagecoach Hill, go north on Route 41.

2.0   Go right on Berkshire School Road 2.8 mi to Route 7.

4.8   Go left on Route 7 for 0.5 miles.

5.3   Go right on County Road, following sign pointing to New Marlboro. Orchard Shade Guest House is on right, the covered bridge is 0.8 miles from Route 7.

11.0   Arrive at triangle intersection where County Road meets Mill River-Great Barrington Road. Go right and head south for 1.7 miles to Mill River General Store.

12.7   After passing store, go right on Clayton Road for 4.0 miles to Henry's Club on left.

16.7   Take right turn opposite Henry's and go over Alum Hill 1.4 miles to Hewins Street.

18.1   Go right on Hewins Street for 3.1 miles to County Road.

21.2   Go left on County Road, through covered bridge, 0.9 miles back to Orchard Shade and Route 7.

22.1   Go left on Route 7, right on Berkshire School Road and left on Route 41 back to Stagecoach Hill, 5.3 miles.

27.4   Stagecoach Hill and total mileage.

Ride 2: Great Barrington Short Loop
10.6 miles

This ride offers one long gradual uphill jaunt from Great Barrington to Monument Mountain, then a long rolling road with lots of scenery, and next a half-mile moderately steep downhill going past the Butternut Basin Ski Area. Other attractions are the Jenifer House, right at the beginning, and the well-kept grounds of the Edward J. Malden Open Heart Memorial on Monument Valley Road.

The ride starts at the McDonald's K-Mart Plaza just north of Great Barrington on Route 7 and heads north on Route 7 to the pass by Monument Mountain, a distance of 3.0 miles and gradually uphill on a main route with wide shoulders. There's a picnic area at the top, affording a dramatic view of the Monument Mountain cliffs where, according to legend, an Indian maiden jumped to her death because of an unhappy love affair.

A few yards north of the picnic area, go right on Monument Valley Road for a delightful 4.6 miles to Route 23. The views are superb, the road is well-paved, and the ride is easy. In fact, it's a near perfect road for bicycling. At Route 23, go right and almost immediately head down a half-mile hill with the Butternut Basin Ski Area on your left, back to Great Barrington for a total distance of 3.1 miles. Make a right on Route 7 and almost immediately you are back to where you started.

Summary: Ride 2

0.0   Start at McDonald's K-Mart Plaza and head north on Route 7.

3.0   Go right on Monument Valley Road and follow south 4.6 miles to Route 23.

7.6   Right on Route 23, 3.1 miles back to Great Barrington, going down half-mile hill by Butternut Basin Ski Area, then right on Route 7 back to start.

10.6 Total mileage.

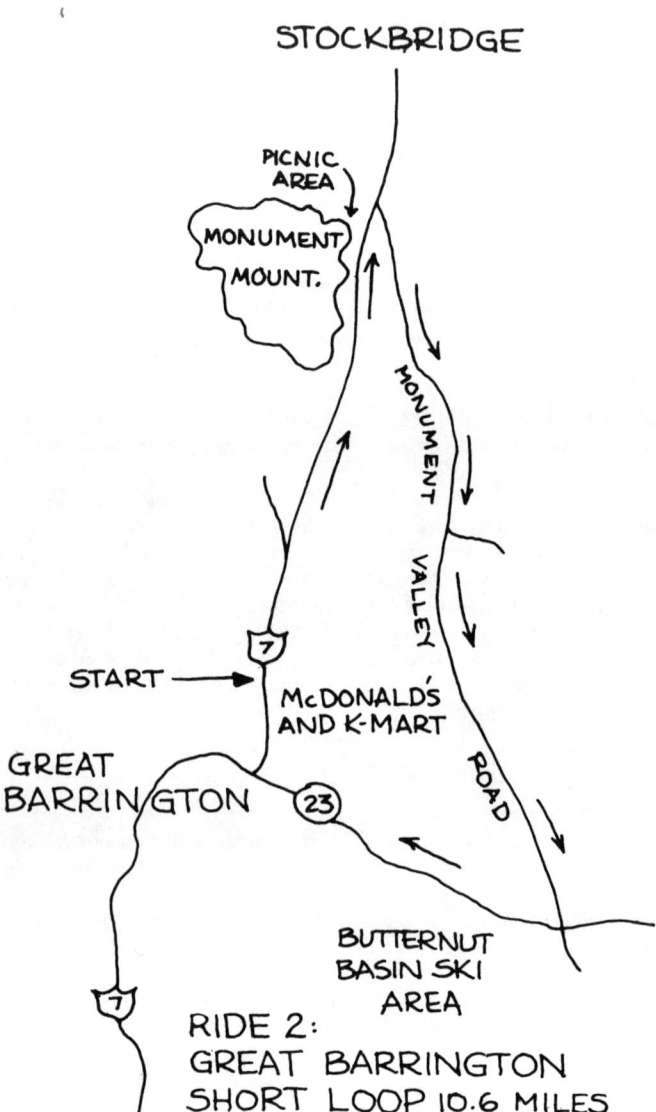

Cliffs on Monument Mountain and rest area are at end of first leg of Great Barrington Short Loop ride, three miles from start.

Ride 3: Great Barrington Long Loop

41.8 miles

This ride has a little bit of everything, including hills, but not mountains. Scenery includes marvelous views of farmscape, a lake, the classic New England village of New Marlboro, and its smaller counterpart, Mill River. Also offered is a sweeping view of Mt. Everett, at 2,624 feet the second highest mountain in the Berkshires, and a generally flat ride for the final one-third.

As in Ride 2, start on Route 7 just north of Great Barrington at the McDonald's K-Mart Plaza and head north up the long gradual hill to Monument Mountain. At the top, make a right on Monument Valley Road just as in Ride 2, but when you arrive at its intersection with Route 23, go left instead of right.

Follow Route 23, a main route with wide shoulders, for 1.2 miles to its intersection with Route 57, where you make a right and head towards New Marlboro. Seven-tenths of a mile from the intersection of Routes 23 and 57, on your right, note the access to Lake Buel, a good spot for a rest stop. Continue southeast on Route 57 for another 1.7 miles and the little village of Hartsville where you keep going straight for another 3.3 miles (a climb with good views and big houses) to New Marlboro, which is dominated by the New Marlboro Meeting House on top of the hill. Its ample lawn also makes a good resting spot, and a plaque by the meeting house provides the visitor with a bit of history.

At this point leave Route 57 by taking a sharp right and follow the sign pointers to Sandisfield and Canaan, Connecticut. The hill goes down for 1.3 miles, then go right on the Mill River-Sandisfield Road, climbing a half-mile hill for a gorgeous view at the top. Descend for another half-mile where the hill flattens and the road continues for 0.6 miles to a T intersection where you go right. Then descend another hill for almost a mile to Mill River, a small village with a general store at its main intersection and an opportunity to take refreshments.

Ride 3 then joins the Ride 1 route, following the bumpy Clayton Road for 4.0 miles bordering the Konkapot River on the left. Look for "Henry's Club" on the left, and take a right on to Alum Hill Road, which begins opposite Henry's,

Built in 1839, the New Marlboro meeting house dominates the village center. Its lawn is inviting for a rest stop.

goes up over a hill, and connects to Hewins Street 1.4 miles later.

Take a right on Hewins Street, but look frequently to the left for magnificent views of Mt. Everett. Follow Hewins Street for 3.1 miles to its intersection with County Road. Take a left, go through the covered bridge and about a mile later meet Route 7. From here on, the ride is mostly flat.

Go left on Route 7 for one-half mile, through the village of Sheffield, then right on Berkshire School Road for 2.8 miles until its intersection with Route 41. Head north on Route 41, crossing the Appalachian Trail marked by a sign 2.5 miles north of the intersection, and then continue another 2.3 miles to the intersection with Route 23 where you go right towards Great Barrington, a distance of 4.0 miles to the intersection of Routes 23 and 7. Follow Route 7 north through the center of Great Barrington for 2.2 miles back to the McDonald's K-Mart Plaza.

Summary: Ride 3

0.0   Start at McDonald's K-Mart Plaza, head north on Route 7.

3.0   Go right on Monument Valley Road and follow south 4.6 miles to Route 23.

7.6   Go left on Route 23 for 1.2 miles to intersection with Route 57.

8.8   Go right on Route 57. At 0.7 miles access to Lake Buel, 2.4 miles to Hartsville and 3.3 to New Marlboro.

15.2   Go right at New Marlboro following signs to Sandisfield and New Canaan, Connecticut, for 1.3 miles.

16.5   Go right on Mill River-Sandisfield Road 1.6 miles to T intersection.

18.1   Go right at T for 1.0 mile to Mill River.

19.1   At Mill River go straight, following Clayton Road for 4.0 miles to Henry's Club.

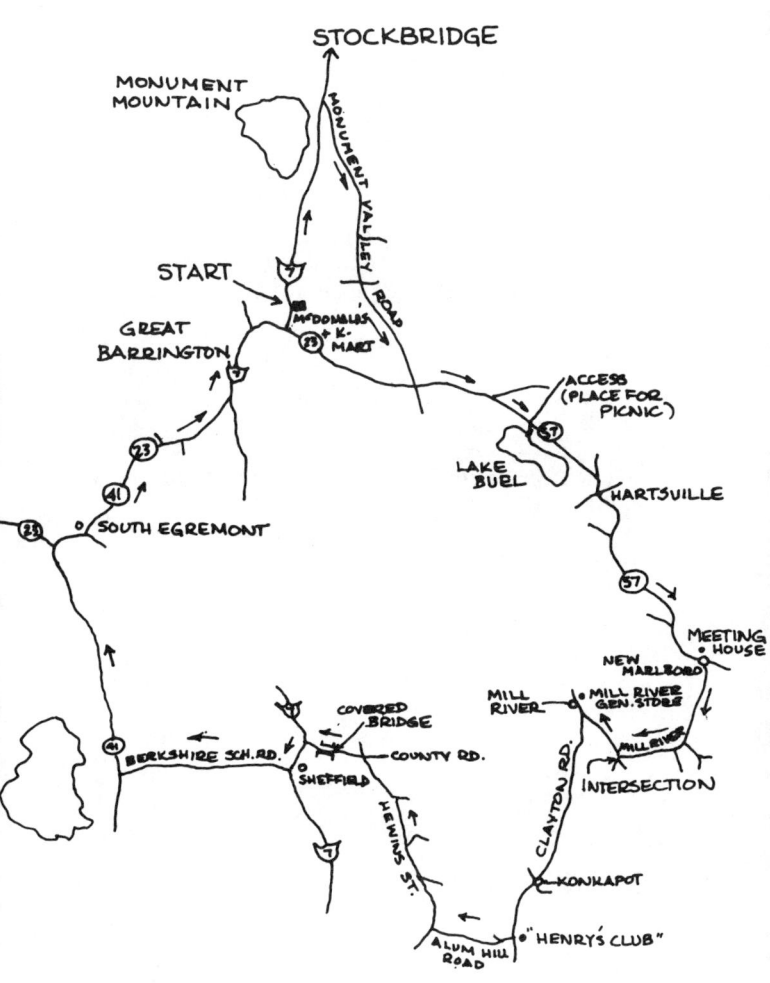

RIDE 3:
GREAT BARRINGTON
LONG LOOP 41.8 MILES

23.1 Take right opposite Henry's and go 1.4 miles up and over Alum Hill.

24.5 Go right on Hewins Street for 3.1 miles to County Road.

27.6 Go left on County Road for 0.9 miles to Route 7.

28.5 Go left on Route 7 for 0.5 miles.

29.0 Go right on Berkshire Schoool Road for 2.8 miles.

31.8 Go right on Route 41 for 3.8 miles.

35.6 Go right at Route 41's intersection with Route 23, following 23 for 4.0 miles.

39.6 Go left on Route 7 for 2.2 miles back to McDonald's K-Mart Plaza.

41.8 Total mileage.

Ride 4: Great Barrington-North Egremont Loop
10.9 miles

This ride is mostly flat with some uphill and a downhill at the end. It offers a particularly good view of Monument Mountain from the south and a side trip may be made to the Albert Schweitzer Friendship House. The trip can be extended a bit by going left on Alford Road to Alford instead of Great Barrington, following the road uphill for a mile to the picturesque town of Alford with its classic white New England style church at the top of the hill. Going right on the Alford Road, as indicated in the trip description, means a downhill all the way back to Great Barrington.

The trip starts at the Southern Berkshire Chamber of Commerce Information Booth on Route 7 immediately south of Great Barrington's central business district. Head south on Route 7 for 0.2 miles and then go right on Route 23 for 1.6 miles, then right on Route 71 for another 1.4 miles to Egremont (an airport is on your right), and next another 2.4 miles straight on Route 71 to North Egremont. All of this part of the ride is delightfully flat.

At North Egremont make a sharp right on Boice Road and climb gradually for 1.7 miles to its intersection with Green River Road where, after pausing for the view of Monument Mountain, the trip goes right, downhill, then up, then down for 1.5 miles to the intersection with Alford Road. Turn right for the trip back to Great Barrington, or if you want to visit the picturesque town of Alford, go left and climb about a mile of gradual hill.

The Albert Schweitzer Friendship Center is about one-half mile on the right from the turn onto Alford Road as the trip heads towards Great Barrington. From the center the trip goes downhill for 1.7 miles back to the information booth.

Summary: Ride 4

0.0   Southern Berkshire Chamber of Commerce Information Booth south on Route 7 for 0.2 miles to Route 23.

0.2   Go right on Route 23 for 1.6 miles.

1.8   Go right on Route 71 for 1.4 miles to Egremont.

3.2 Go straight at Egremont on Route 71 for another 2.4 miles to North Egremont.

5.6 Go right on Boice Road for 1.7 miles to intersection with Green River Road.

7.3 Go right on Green River Road for 1.5 miles to intersection with Alford Road.

8.8 Go right on Alford Road back to information center, 2.1 miles.

10.9 Total mileage.

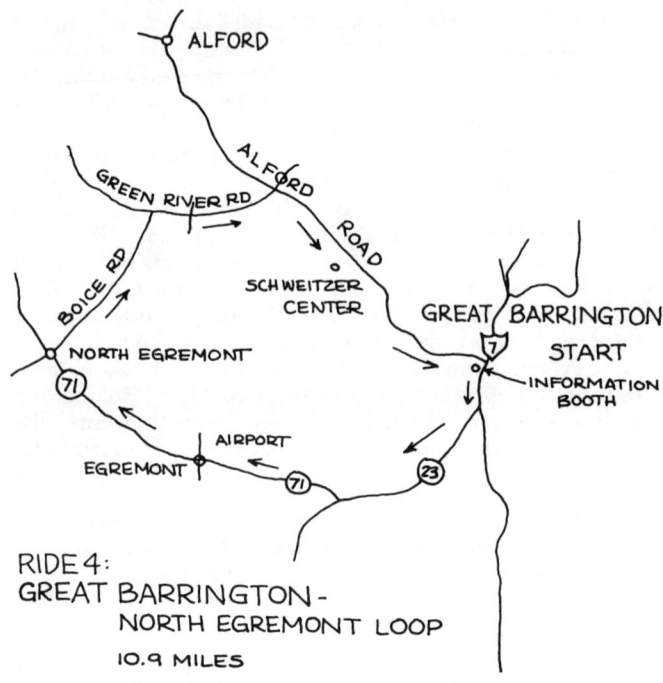

RIDE 4:
GREAT BARRINGTON –
NORTH EGREMONT LOOP
10.9 MILES

Ride 4, the Great Barrington-North Egremont Loop, begins at the Southern Berkshire Chamber of Commerce Information Booth on Route 7.

Ride 5: Great Barrington-West Stockbridge Loop
28.2 miles

This ride offers a gradual climb from Great Barrington to West Stockbridge, a town that is experiencing an interesting rebirth, and then a return route along the western border of the county through the town of Alford, a way offering unusually beautiful views of farmland.

Both West Stockbridge and Alford are interesting for different reasons. Until the early 1970s West Stockbridge's history was primarily influenced by its location as a gateway to the western central part of the county, first because of the Hudson and Berkshire Railroad, whose way was laid out in 1838, and more recently because of the Massachusetts Turnpike, whose Interchange No. 1 is just south of the business district. In the early days the Williams River, which runs through the town, augmented commerce as a source of power for grist mills. Quarrying operations also took place in the surrounding hills in West Stockbridge's early days.

In 1973 a New York developer bought most of the old business buildings between Main Street and the river and then refurbished them for rental to craftspeople in a major effort to transform the town into a center for selling craftwork. The effort has had some major problems, but the results are obviously productive as both old-style and newer businesses share the Main Street space.

Alford, about 10 miles south of West Stockbridge, is a classic New England village with its well-defined center of a church, town hall, schoolhouse and residences. The open agricultural area surrounding the town stands as testimony to the value of farmland for scenery since it is reported that about 60 percent of the land in the town is owned by New Yorkers.

The ride starts at the McDonald's K-Mart Plaza on Route 7 just north of Great Barrington and proceeds south on Route 7 for 1.2 miles to its intersection with Route 41, where it makes a sharp right, leaving Route 7 and heading north on Route 41, first climbing a hill and then opening out onto a flat section with pretty views on both sides.

The ride continues through the little village of Williamsville, with a rest stop recommended at the Williamsville Inn, one of the county's older country lodging

Alford, with its church and other similar classic structures, is one of the more picturesque small villages in the Berkshires.

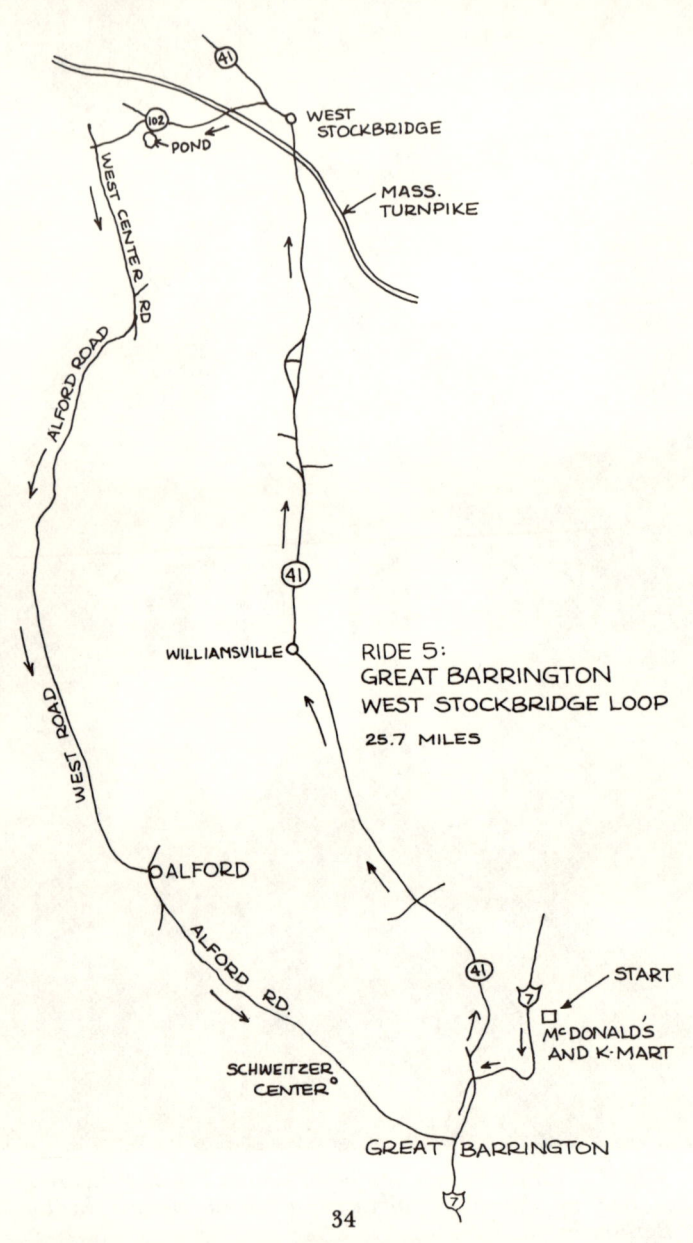

places. Climb the half-mile from Williamsville and then proceed along the very gradual uphill to West Stockbridge, a total of about 11 miles from the ride's start.

Make a left on Route 102 in West Stockbridge, heading west on Main Street, then make another left at its end, crossing the river and passing the Old Shaker Mill, an antiques place, on the left. Continue on Route 102 past where Route 41 bears off to the right, go over the Massachusetts Turnpike and then go left at a small pond 1.9 miles from the West Stockbridge Center at West Center Road. Follow this road for 3.0 miles to a T intersection where the ride goes right on Alford Road and 4.9 miles to the center of Alford. The roads from West Stockbridge thread their way through some of the more magnificent farm scenery in the county.

At Alford go left (actually, because of a triangle, going left means going left twice) and head downhill for 2.6 miles to the Albert Schweitzer Friendship Center and another 1.7 miles to the intersection with Route 7 in Great Barrington. Turn left on Route 7, go through the Great Barrington business district and follow Route 7 north to the McDonald's K-Mart Plaza, a distance of 1.9 miles.

Summary: Ride 5

0.0 From McDonald's K-Mart Plaza, go south on Route 7 1.2 miles to intersection with Route 41.

1.2 Go right, following Route 41 11 miles to intersection with Route 102 in West Stockbridge.

12.2 Go left on Route 102 following it for 1.9 miles until left turn at West Center Road.

14.1 Follow West Center Road for three miles.

17.1 Go right on Alford Road at T intersection for 4.9 miles.

22.0 Go left at Alford for 4.3 miles to Route 7 in Great Barrington.

26.3 Go right on Route 7 for 1.9 miles back to start.

28.2 Total mileage.

Ride 6: West Stockbridge-Pittsfield Loop

22.6 miles
(Can also be done from Pittsfield)

Although there's a steady climb from West Stockbridge to Pittsfield on Route 41, a distance of 8.7 miles, this is generally a flat ride, providing good scenery, especially on Barker Road from Pittsfield south to West Stockbridge. One of the ride's main attractions is its potential for visiting the Hancock Shaker Village, just off the intersection of Routes 20 and 41, or the ease from which it can be done from downtown Pittsfield.

The ride starts by taking Route 41 out of West Stockbridge, bearing right where Route 102 separates and heading north through the largely rural, residential town of Richmond to Route 41's intersection with Route 20. Approaching Route 20, on the right, riders will see Richmond Pond. Just after Richmond Pond, on the left, the buildings comprising Hancock Shaker Village, including the round barn, can be seen. Entrance to the Shaker Village is from Route 20 by going left at the intersection.

Heading right on Route 20 eventually leads to Pittsfield's downtown, 4.6 miles away. The road back to West Stockbridge, Barker Road, is 3.6 miles from the Routes 41 and 20 intersection and has a traffic light as additional identification.

Turn right on Barker Road for a 9.8 mile ride back to West Stockbridge through rolling farmland and residences.

If the ride is taken from Pittsfield, the trip starts at Park Square, follows Route 7 south for 0.2 miles to the Route 20 (Housatonic Street) turnoff, where a right is made. Follow Housatonic Street for 0.8 miles to its intersection with Barker Road, marked by a traffic light. Turn left on Barker Road for the 9.8 mile ride to West Stockbridge.

Ride 6 goes right by the Hancock Shaker Village, a museum that can provide a destination focus for this trip or for the one described in Ride 15.

The village is one of 19 settlements established in the 18th century by the Shakers, a religious sect that believed in communal living, spartan life and the concept that form follows function. Eighteen of the 22 buildings in the village have been carefully restored, including a round stone barn, con-

West Stockbridge is experiencing a rebirth as craft-oriented businesses have moved into its old commercial buildings.

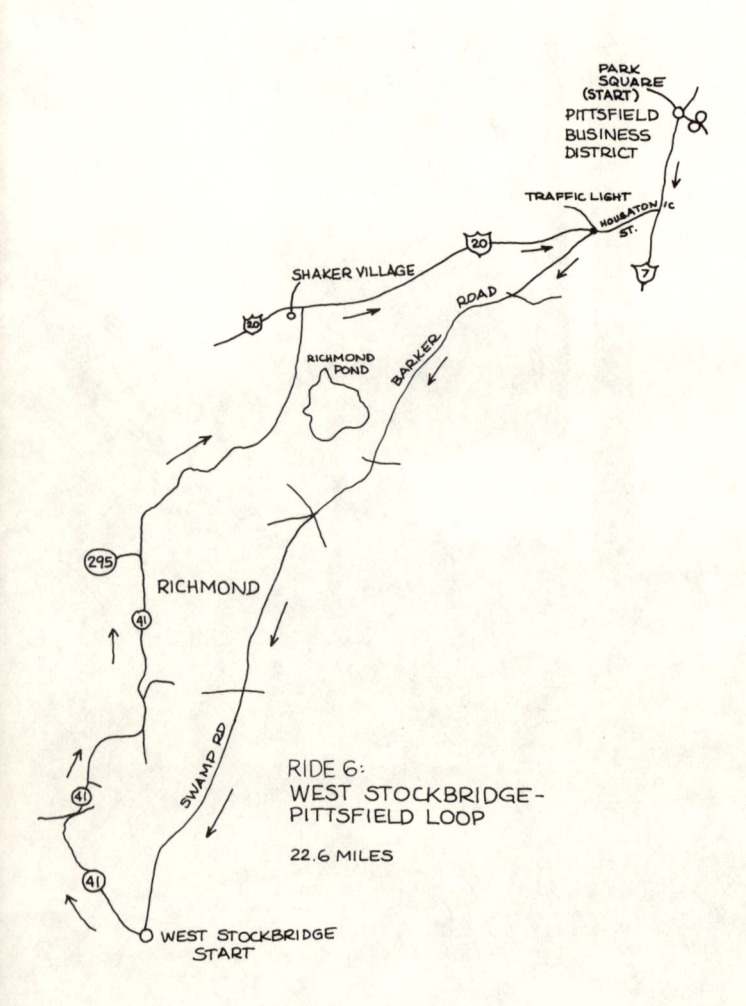

sidered the most important building architecturally. The barn was designed to allow one man to feed an entire herd of cattle because each animal faced inward in a circle of stanchions. Other buildings also have furniture and other arrangements that reflect the Shakers' constant effort to seek more efficient ways of doing things.

The museum is open daily, 9:30 a.m. to 5 p.m., June 1 to Nov. 1. Admission is $3.50 adults, $1 children.

Summary: Ride 6

0.0   Start in middle of West Stockbridge and head west on Routes 41 and 102, staying on Route 41 when it heads north for 8.7 miles until its intersection with Route 20.

8.7   Go right on Route 20 (left for Shaker Village) for 3.6 miles to its intersection with Barker Road on right at traffic light.

12.3   Follow Barker Road (it becomes Swamp Road in Lenox) for 9.8 miles back to West Stockbridge.

22.1   Total mileage.

If starting from Park Square, Pittsfield:

0.0   From Park Square head south on Route 7 for 0.2 miles to intersection with Route 20 (Housatonic Street).

0.2   Go right on Housatonic Street for 0.8 miles to intersection with Barker Road.

1.0   Go left on Barker Road 9.8 miles to West Stockbridge.

10.8   At West Stockbridge, head west on Routes 102 and 41, staying on Route 41 when it heads north for 8.7 miles until its intersection with Route 20.

19.5   Go right on Route 20 for 4.6 miles back to Route 7 and Park Square.

24.1   Total mileage.

The Curtis Hotel dominates the center of Lenox.

Chapter 3:
Estates and Industry:
Stockbridge, Lenox and Housatonic

In many respects Rides 7 through 16 described in this chapter offer the most interesting glimpses of the impact the late 19th century history in America had on the towns of Lenox, Stockbridge and Housatonic. The first two were watering places for the aristocracy of a gilded age, and the third, a classic New England mill town, still has an appearance little altered from its more prosperous days.

During the early and mid-19th century a number of famous authors wrote from places in the Berkshires. At one time or another their ranks included William Cullen Bryant, Catherine Sedgwick, Nathaniel Hawthorne, Oliver Wendell Holmes, Henry Wadsworth Longfellow, Henry Ward Beecher, Henry David Thoreau and Herman Melville. Their writing included rapturous descriptions of Berkshire scenery, especially in the area around Stockbridge, Lenox and south of Pittsfield. At the same time, the industrial revolution in America had created huge fortunes, with the result that wealthy people, attracted by the writings of these well-known authors, began to visit the Berkshires, and then establish themselves in estates around Lenox and Stockbridge.

The estates were planned with careful attention to obtain the maximum view of Monument Mountain, the Stockbridge Bowl or other attractive features of the landscape. The estate owners also contributed their talents to improving the beauty of Stockbridge and Lenox by laying out wide streets, planting trees along them and providing for lawns between the sidewalks and roads.

In a very real sense, by 1900 the Stockbridge-Lenox area had developed into a huge park, dotted with rolling lawns, ponds, imaginatively shaped trees, curving walks and carefully manicured grounds. That kind of lifestyle no longer exists but the effects can be seen in the Lenox-Stockbridge area where former estates have become schools, museums, music centers, or galleries.

The village of Housatonic has a different story, one much more directly connected to the industrial revolution and the use of water power. The Housatonic River, flowing down from Stockbridge, Lee and Pittsfield, supplied power for two major mills, Monument Mills in the center of town, now a modern ruin, and what is now the Rising Paper Company just south of Housatonic. The village itself is laid out in the typical mill town pattern, with houses and businesses clustered around the river that runs between two mountains.

Monument Mills closed in the early 1950s, and its gutted hulk now looms gloomily over the town, a harsh reminder of changing times. The Rising Paper Company is startling in its Victorian architecture, with four stories and two towers rising majestically behind tall spruce trees along Route 183 and the river flowing along its other side, coursing through a dam just above the mill. When built in 1876 the mill was the largest paper plant in the world.

Route 183 winds its way through the history of all three towns, beginning in Housatonic and then following the river, at times rough with rapids, passing just north of the Stockbridge business district to end in Lenox after going by Tanglewood and other estates. The road rolls with the land, seldom intruding on its natural features and allowing the rider to contemplate the 19th century conditions that shaped the histories of these three towns.

Most of the rides start at the Red Lion Inn in Stockbridge, a traditional country lodging place. The inn, perhaps the most famous of its kind in New England, has 90 rooms, a spacious front porch, indoor and outdoor dining, a cozy tavern, an inviting hearth and many other amenities for the traveller, whether on bicycle or otherwise.

Nowhere else can the county boast such a concentration of cultural offerings as in the Stockbridge-Lenox area. The following list represents thumbnail sketches of major attractions in the area and the rides that include them on their routes.

Arrowhead, Pittsfield: Ride 16.

Herman Melville, the author of Moby Dick, moved to the Berkshires in 1850 where he lived for 13 years at Arrowhead, then a farm and now the headquarters of the Berkshire County Historical Society at 780 Holmes Road, Pittsfield.

During the 1850s Nathaniel Hawthorne lived six miles away in Lenox, and Oliver Wendell Holmes a mile away. All three authors were friends. Much of Arrowhead has been restored. Furnished with period pieces, the house contains valuable memorabilia about its most famous owner. It is open May 1 to Oct. 31, weekdays, 10 to 5 p.m., Sundays, 1 to 5 p.m., and is closed Tuesdays. Admission is $1 adults, 50 cents for students.

Berkshire Garden Center, Stockbridge: Rides 8, 9, 10, 11, 13

Approximately at the intersection of Routes 102 and 183, just northwest of Stockbridge, the center's offerings include beautiful gardens, a solar heated greenhouse, lily ponds, herbs, youth programs, exhibits, lectures, workshops and a gift shop.

Berkshire Playhouse, Stockbridge: Ride 9.

While Ride 9 is the only one that goes directly by the Berkshire Playhouse, which is at the foot of Yale Hill, the theater is only about a 10-minute walk from the Red Lion Inn. Ask anybody for directions. The second oldest summer theater in the United States, it operates three performance facilities on its grounds during the July and August season.

Chesterwood, Stockbridge: Rides 8, 11, 13.

Sculptor Daniel Chester French is best known for his Seated Lincoln statue in Washington, D.C. and his Minute Man at Concord. He came to Stockbridge in 1896 and for three decades created sculpture from a studio exactingly planned for its special function. The estate is both a National Historic Landmark and Massachusetts Historic Landmark. Its offerings include memorabilia, a gallery and a museum shop. It is open daily, 10 a.m. to 5 p.m., May 1 to Oct. 31. Admission is charged.

Crane Museum, Dalton: Ride 16. (Also Ride 17 in Ch 4).

The Crane Paper Company in Dalton makes all the paper on which U.S. currency is printed and also manufactures other quality lines of paper. The one-room museum, on Route 9, is made from an early mill and through models, photos and paper samples tells how fine paper is made. The museum is open June through September from Monday to Friday, 2 to 5 p.m. Admission is free.

Hancock Shaker Village, Hancock: Ride 15.

The village is described in a special note accompanying Ride 6, Chapter 2.

The main street of Stockbridge is a bustle of activity during the summer months.

Mission House, Stockbridge: Rides 7, 8, 9, 10, 11.

The Mission House on Main Street, Stockbridge, is the former home of the Rev. John Sergeant, first missionary to the Stockbridge Indians. The story of the Rev. Mr. Sergeant, his bride and the house is fascinating, but too long to tell here. The authentic colonial furnishings reflect the separate interests of Sergeant and his wife. The gardens are especially interesting. The house is open May 28 to Oct. 15, Tuesday through Saturday from 10 a.m. to 5 p.m., and Sunday 11 a.m. to 5 p.m. Admission, $1.25 adults, 25 cents children under 14.

Naumkeag, Stockbridge: Rides 10, 12.

Naumkeag, the summer home of Joseph H. Choate, lawyer for the Rockefeller family and once ambassador to the Court of St. James, provides a glimpse of the kinds of lavish estates that made the Stockbridge-Lenox area famous. Elegant, unusual, fantastic are all words that could apply to the estate. Naumkeag is open during the summer, Tuesday through Saturday from 10 a.m. to 5 p.m., Sundays and holidays 11 a.m. to 4 p.m. Admissions range from 50 cents to $2.

Old Corner House, Stockbridge: Rides 7, 8, 9, 10, 11.

Only minutes away from the Red Lion Inn, the Old Corner House has the only permanent collection of Norman Rockwell paintings on public display in the United States, including many Saturday Evening Post covers. Mr. Rockwell, perhaps the nation's best known illustrator, lived in Stockbridge from 1953 until his death in 1978. The Corner House is open daily from 10 to 5 p.m. and closed Tuesdays, Thanksgiving, Christmas and New Year's Day. Admission, $1 adults, 25 cents children under 12.

Pleasant Valley Sanctuary and Canoe Meadows, Lenox.

No rides in this guide go directly by the Pleasant Valley Sanctuary because its entrance is off busy Route 7 opposite the Holiday Inn between Lenox and Pittsfield. Yet the sanctuary is worth mentioning because of its proximity to Lenox and because of its extensive nature walks, its small trailside museum and live exhibits of native plants, fish, snakes and other animals. Pleasant Valley and its less developed counterpart, Canoe Meadows, off Holmes Road in Pittsfield, are maintained by the Massachusetts Audubon Society. The sanctuary is open daily, sunrise to sunset, admission $1 for adults, free for children and for members of the Audubon Society.

Shakespeare and Company, Lenox.

No rides go directly by The Mount on Plunkett Road, home of Shakespeare & Company, but it bears mention because it is a company of Shakespearean actors founded in 1978 that performs weekend evenings on the grounds in July and August. The location is the summer place of Edith Wharton, an American novelist who died in 1937.

Stritch Sculpture Gardens, Hinsdale: Ride 16. (Also Ride 17 in Chapter 4).

John Stritch is a sculptor who works in metal, welding together all sorts of new and used metal to create a variety of sculpture. His works dot the grounds of his studio on Route 143, one-half mile east of Route 8 in Hinsdale.

Tanglewood, Lenox: Rides 9, 10, 13, 14.

A lovely 210-acre estate that overlooks the Stockbridge Bowl in Tanglewood has been the permanent summer home of the Boston Symphony Orchestra since 1936. Major concerts are given on Friday and Saturday evenings and Sunday afternoons during July and August, many of them under the direction of guest conductors. In addition, there are other offerings, including open rehearsals of the B.S.O. and concerts by musicians of the Berkshire Music Center. Tanglewood draws about 250,000 visitors to its programs each summer, and as such is a major tourist offering in the Berkshires. Even without a concert the grounds are worth a visit. During concerts, they draw hundreds of picnickers who can sit on the lawn at a reduced admission. Any bicyclist who wants to tour in and around Tanglewood on a Sunday afternoon in July and August had better be prepared for extremely heavy traffic.

Tyringham Art Galleries and Gingerbread House, Tyringham: Ride 12.

Slightly off the beaten path for most tourists are the Tyringham galleries and Gingerbread House, the former studio of Sir Henry Hudson Kitson, the sculptor who created the Minute Man at Lexington. The building is unusual and the works inside are mostly modern American.

Ride 7: Stockbridge-Cherry Hill Challenge
4.3 miles

This is a pretty ride offering a glimpse of some of the residential areas of Stockbridge as well as a short traverse of the Stockbridge Golf Club, one of the better courses in the east. The ride is good, either for a leisurely morning or afternoon, or for a warm-up before a longer trip and the chance to adjust gears. The route is hilly, but the hills are short.

The ride starts at the Red Lion Inn and follows Route 102 west for 0.4 miles to the cluster of scenic buildings that includes the First Congregational Church, the Stockbridge Chime Tower and the Stockbridge Town Hall. Route 102 goes right, but this ride continues straight, crossing the Stockbridge Golf Club and then the Housatonic River, bearing to the right after the bridge.

From the Housatonic, start the climb up Cherry Hill, going straight at the sign pointing right to Chesterwood, and going straight after the bridge over the railroad tracks. In about one-half mile the road goes straight over a railroad crossing. Turn left on Cherry Hill Road, just before the crossing, climb a hill for 0.2 miles and then coast downhill for another 0.4 miles until a T intersection. Go left at the T, continue for another climb of about 0.4 miles where there's a small triangle intersection. Go right, and down a hill for 0.5 miles to the intersection of Cherry Hill Road with Goodrich Street. Turn left on Goodrich Street and follow it for one-half mile to its intersection with Route 7. Turn left on Route 7 for the 0.6 mile trip back to the Red Lion Inn.

Summary: Ride 7

0.0 Start at Red Lion Inn and follow Route 102 west for 0.4 miles where Congregational Church and Town Hall are on your left and Route 102 goes right.

0.4 Go straight ahead, dipping down a small hill, crossing Stockbridge golf course and bridge over Housatonic, then bearing right and going straight, past sign to Chesterwood, taking bridge over tracks for total of 1.3 miles to rail crossing.

Most of the Stockbridge rides start at the Red Lion Inn, one of the more famous lodgings of its type in New England.

1.7   Go left before crossing tracks, climb hill for 0.2 miles, then go downhill for 0.4 miles until a T intersection.

2.3   Go left at T intersection for 0.4 miles up hill.

2.7   At top of hill, go right at little triangle, and down hill for 0.5 miles to Goodrich Street.

3.2   Go left on Goodrich Street for 0.5 miles to intersection with Route 7.

3.7   Go left on Route 7 for 0.6 miles back to Red Lion Inn.

4.3   Total mileage.

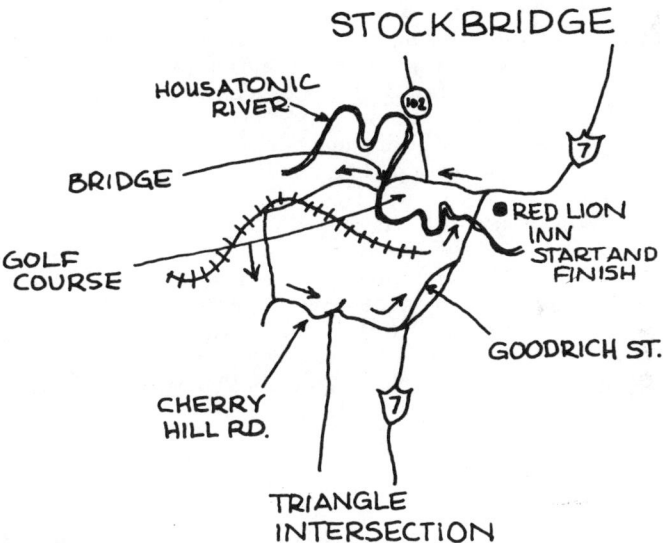

RIDE 7:
STOCKBRIDGE -
CHERRY HILL CHALLENGE 4.3 MILES

Ride 8: Stockbridge-Housatonic Loop, and
Ride 9: Stockbridge-Lenox Loop

Can be ridden separately or together. If ridden together the total mileage is 25.6. One suggestion is to make them a morning and afternoon ride, with lunch at the Red Lion Inn.

Ride 8: Stockbridge-Housatonic Loop

10.6 miles if linked with Ride 9.
12.5 miles if loop is completed.

Start at the Red Lion Inn and head south on Route 7, a main road with good shoulders, for four miles, climbing gradually for about two miles to the crest of the pass beside Monument Mountain, where there's a picnic area and an impressive close-up view of Monument Mountain's cliffs. It was here, legend has it, that an Indian maiden jumped to her death because of an unhappy love affair.

Ride downhill for nearly a mile, taking a right at a sign about halfway down the hill that points to Route 183 "Housatonic — 3; Interlaken — 8." Follow that road for 0.4 miles and then go right on Route 183, pedaling 1.2 miles to the Rising Paper Mill on your left with its expansive "mill pond," the dammed up Housatonic, just beyond. You have another 1.1 miles to the village of Housatonic.

Follow Route 183 through Housatonic, taking a right after the bridge over the Housatonic River to start climbing gradually. The first impressive view, almost immediately, is the ruin of the Monument Mountain mill on the right. The second is the stretch of Housatonic, with its lively rapids, that goes along the road on the right for about two miles. Further up the road on the right will be seen a small abandoned hydroelectric plant that for a brief period supplied power to the Monument Mountain mill.

The turnoff to Chesterwood, the summer house of the sculptor Daniel Chester French, is 3.3 miles north of Housatonic, and the ride to the grounds is about a half-mile up a slight hill. About a mile beyond the Chesterwood turnoff Route 183 intersects with Route 102.

If you want to return to the Red Lion Inn from the intersection, take a right and follow Route 102 southeast 1.5 miles to the Stockbridge Chime Tower, the Stockbridge

When built in 1876, this mill in Housatonic was the largest paper plant in the world. Now the home of the Rising Paper Co.

Town Hall and the First Congregational Church, a beautiful cluster of buildings. At this point turn left on Route 102 at the T intersection and ride 0.4 flat miles back to the Red Lion Inn.

Ride 9: Stockbridge-Lenox Loop

16.9 miles if started from Stockbridge.
15 miles if continued from Ride 8.

The ride starts at the Red Lion Inn and heads west on Route 102 past the Stockbridge Town Hall, Chime Tower and the First Congregational Church where Route 102 takes a right and the road goes 1.5 miles up to the intersection of Route 183, the end of Ride 8. Here make a right turn and follow Route 183 towards Lenox, going underneath the Massachusetts Turnpike overpass and through the picturesque village of Interlaken. Approximately 2.5 miles from the intersection of Routes 102 and 183, after a gradual uphill climb, the rider will begin to catch glimpses of the Stockbridge Bowl. There is public access to the Bowl through an ample parking lot at 3.1 miles from the Routes 102 and 183 intersection, a fine place for a picnic and for small boat watching on a summer day.

The ride continues north on Route 183 and reaches the main gate of Tanglewood on the right in another 1.1 miles. A bit of gradual climbing after Tanglewood brings the trip to Lenox at the large intersection of Routes 7A and 183, the doorstep of the Curtis Hotel.

From the Curtis Hotel, follow Route 7A south to Route 7 for 1.5 miles and then continue south along Route 7, a major travelled way, for 2.5 miles, where the sign to High Lawn Farm can be spotted on the left. Go past the High Lawn Farm sign on Route 7 for another 0.6 miles and then take an oblique left from Route 7. Unfortunately the left is not marked, but it is the first left after the High Lawn Farm sign. If the turn is missed, don't worry because Route 7 takes you back to Stockbridge and the ride's start.

Assuming you've made the turn, you are now on West Road. Follow it for 0.9 miles until the first stop sign, at the intersection of West and Devon Roads. Go straight and ride for another 0.8 miles to the second stop sign, this time at West and Stockbridge Roads. Go straight through. West becomes Church Street, a relatively steep downhill for one

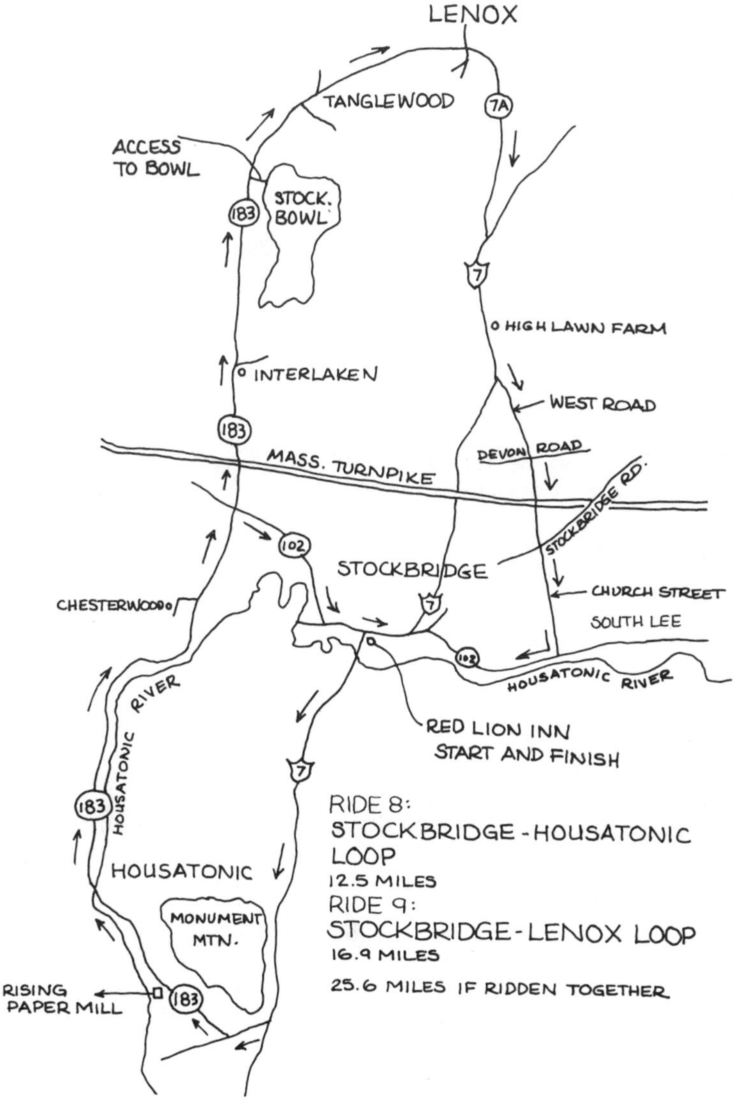
LENOX
TANGLEWOOD
7A
ACCESS TO BOWL
STOCK. BOWL
183
7
HIGH LAWN FARM
INTERLAKEN
WEST ROAD
183
DEVON ROAD
MASS. TURNPIKE
STOCKBRIDGE RD.
102
STOCKBRIDGE
CHESTERWOOD
7
CHURCH STREET
SOUTH LEE
102
HOUSATONIC RIVER
RIVER
HOUSATONIC
RED LION INN
START AND FINISH
7
183
HOUSATONIC
MONUMENT MTN.
RISING PAPER MILL
183
RIDE 8:
STOCKBRIDGE-HOUSATONIC LOOP
12.5 MILES
RIDE 9:
STOCKBRIDGE-LENOX LOOP
16.9 MILES
25.6 MILES IF RIDDEN TOGETHER

mile to the road's intersection with Route 102. Go right on Route 102 for an easy two-mile ride back to the Red Lion Inn.

Summary: Ride 8

0.0   Start at Red Lion Inn and go south 4.0 miles on Route 7. Climb hill to Monument Mountain, then on downhill side spot sign pointing to Route 183, Housatonic and Interlaken.

4.0   Go right at sign for 0.4 miles.

4.4   Go right on Route 183, following it 6.2 miles to intersection with Route 102.

10.6   Continue straight for Ride 9. Go right on Route 102 for 1.9 miles back to Red Lion Inn.

12.5   Total mileage.

Summary: Ride 9

0.0   Either start at Red Lion Inn following Route 102 west for 1.9 miles to intersection with Route 183 or continue from Ride 8. The 0.0 is where Routes 183 and 102 intersect. Follow Route 183 for 3.1 miles and public access to Stockbridge Bowl on right.

3.1   At Stockbridge Bowl stop for picnic or keep going straight, 1.1 miles to Tanglewood main gate and another 1.5 miles to Lenox Center and Curtis Hotel.

5.7   At Curtis Hotel go south on Route 7A for 1.5 miles to intersection with Route 7.

7.2   Go south on Route 7 for 2.5 miles, looking for sign for High Lawn Farm on left, then another 0.6 miles for oblique left going off Route 7, the first left after High Lawn sign.

10.3 Follow West Road (the oblique left) for 0.9 miles to first stop sign. Go straight for 0.8 miles to second stop sign. Go straight on Church Street for 1.0 miles to intersection with Route 102.

13.0 Go right on Route 102 back to Red Lion Inn. 2.0 miles.

15.0 Total mileage Ride 9. Total mileage Rides 8 and 9, 25.6.

Ride 10: Stockbridge Bowl Ride-Around
11.3 miles

This ride is not only pretty, it takes the visitor by most of the major attractions in the Stockbridge-Lenox area, including estates, the Old Corner House, Mission House, within a stone's throw of the Berkshire Garden Center, Tanglewood, the Stockbridge Bowl itself and Naumkeag.

The ride starts at the Red Lion Inn and heads west on Route 102 for 0.4 miles and the scenic cluster of buildings that includes the Stockbridge Town Hall, the Stockbridge Chime Tower and the First Congregational Church. Turn right, following Route 102 for 1.5 miles to its intersection with Route 183 where the ride again turns right.

Route 183 goes under the Massachusetts Turnpike and through the quaint village of Interlaken, climbing gradually to the Stockbridge Bowl and a public access way 3.1 miles from the intersection of Routes 102 and 183. This is a good place for a picnic, but before deciding consider what lies another half-mile ahead.

From the access, continue on Route 183 for another 0.8 miles and make a right at Hawthorne Street, the south border of the Tanglewood grounds and the second good spot for a picnic because the view overlooks the bowl with Monument Mountain in the background. It's one of the more famous panoramas in the Berkshires. If it's a Sunday afternoon in July or August the Boston Symphony Orchestra will be playing, adding to the ambience of the surroundings. One word of warning, though. Traffic around Tanglewood on a Sunday afternoon when the orchestra is playing is apt to be heavy.

Continue the ride on Hawthorne Street. At 0.7 miles from Route 183 Hawthorne Street goes left to Lenox. The ride goes straight for another 4.8 miles, with the Bowl on the right and then a final two mile descent of Prospect Hill. Bear right near the bottom and the ride comes out directly opposite the Red Lion Inn.

The ride can also begin in Lenox, starting at the Curtis Hotel and then heading down Stockbridge Road for 0.3 miles, then right at Hawthorne Street and down a 1.5 mile hill to the stop sign. Go left for 4.8 miles to Stockbridge,

Tanglewood's main entrance, off Route 183, is dominated by majestic trees in view from the road.

RIDE 10: STOCKBRIDGE BOWL RIDE-AROUND
11.3 MILES

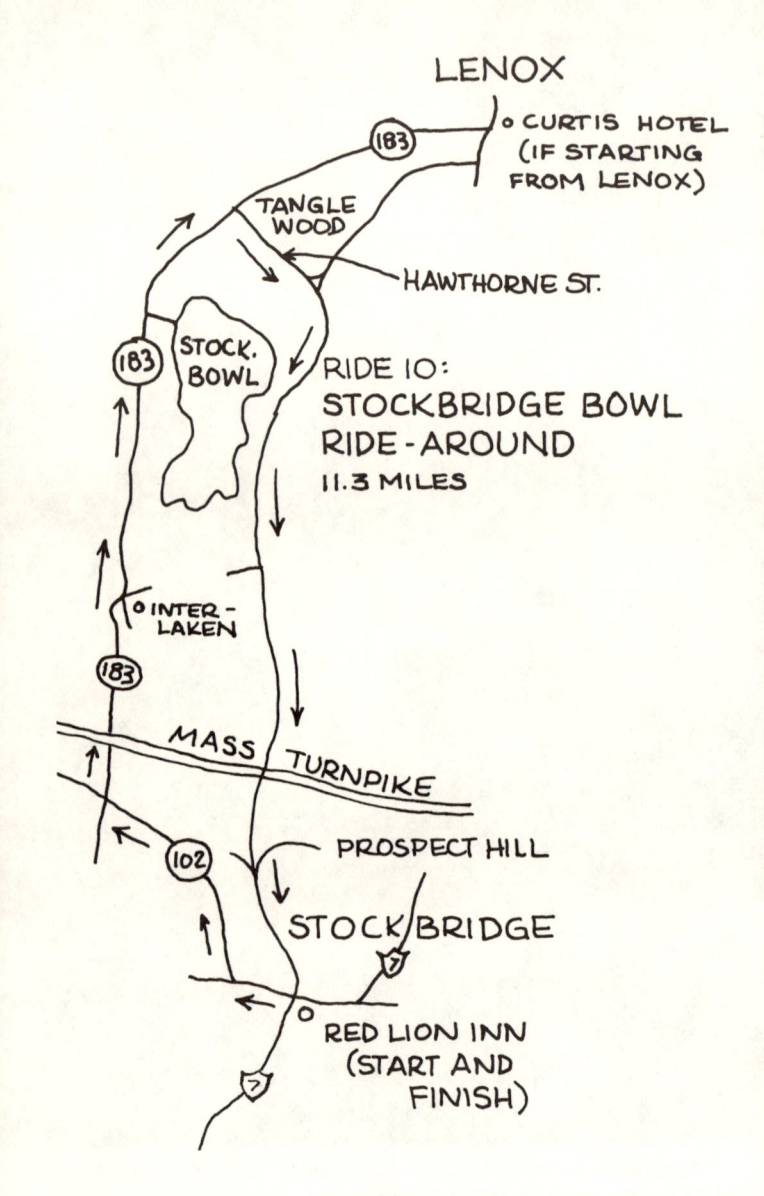

picking up the ride at the 0.0 mark.

To avoid the final hill going back to Lenox, stay on Route 183 instead of going right on Hawthorne Street just before Tanglewood. From Hawthorne Street to Lenox Center on Route 183 is 1.7 miles.

Summary: Ride 10

0.0   From Red Lion Inn, head west on Route 102 for 0.4 miles then follow it right for 1.5 miles to intersection with Route 183.

1.9   Go right on Route 183, following it 3.1 miles to access to Stockbridge Bowl, and another 0.8 miles to Hawthorne Street.

5.8   Go right on Hawthorne Street, following it for 0.7 miles until it turns left for Lenox. Go straight for another 4.8 miles back to Stockbridge.

11.3   Total mileage.

If taken from Lenox add about 3.5 miles to total mileage.

Ride 11: Stockbridge-Chesterwood-Berkshire Garden Center

6 miles

This ride includes visits to two of the Stockbridge area's chief attractions. The first is Chesterwood, the summer home of sculptor Daniel Chester French (1850-1931), creator of "Seated Lincoln" in Washington D.C. and the "Minute Man" in Concord, Massachusetts. The second is the Berkshire Garden Center, a center of information about gardening and solar greenhouses.

The ride begins at the Red Lion Inn and heads west on Route 102, going straight where Route 102 takes a right. On the left is a picturesque cluster of buildings that includes the First Congregational Church, the Stockbridge Town Hall and the Stockbridge Chime Tower. The road straight ahead takes a gradual left over a section of the Stockbridge golf course, then goes over the Housatonic River where the ride bears right and climbs a hill. At a mile from the ride's beginning, on the right, a sign points to Chesterwood. Take the right according to the sign's direction and follow the winding road uphill 0.7 miles up to its intersection with Route 183, where the ride goes left.

Follow Route 183 for 0.2 miles to another Chesterwood sign, go right for 0.1 miles and then left for 0.5 miles, up another hill that turns into a dirt road just before Chesterwood.

On the return from Chesterwood take a left on Route 183, following it north for 1.0 flat miles to its intersection with Route 102. Take a left on Route 102 and the Berkshire Garden Center is almost immediately on your right.

To go back to Stockbridge, take Route 102 south for 1.6 miles, following it as it goes left at the First Congregational Church for another 0.4 miles back to the Red Lion Inn.

Even though none of the hills in the first part of this ride are very long, they can be avoided by making the trip a linear one instead of a loop. To do this, take Route 102 west from the Red Lion Inn, go left on Route 183 to Chesterwood and return the same way. The total mileage of the linear trip is 7.1 miles, a mile longer but less hilly.

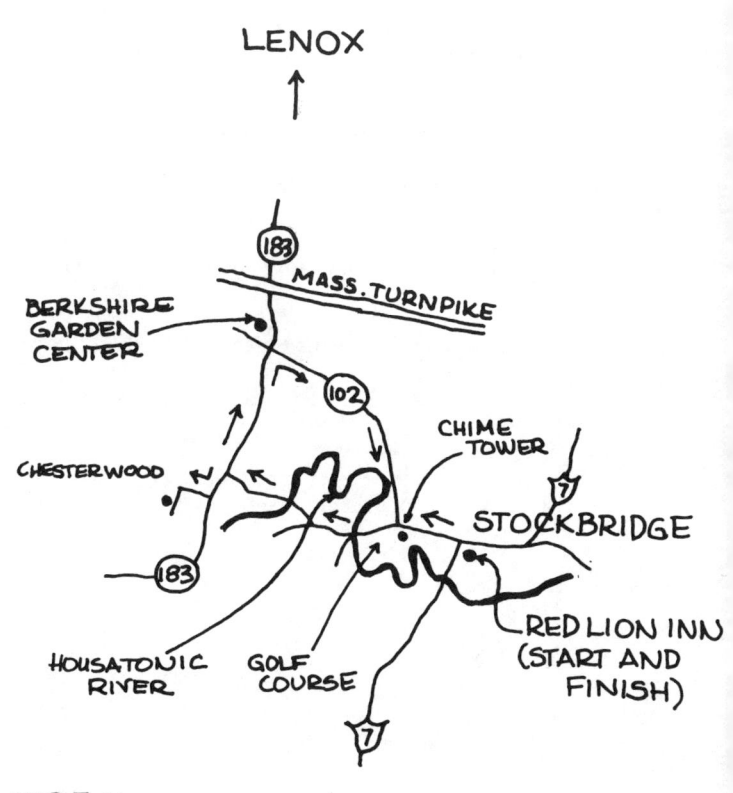

RIDE 11:
STOCKBRIDGE / CHESTERWOOD /
BERKSHIRE GARDEN CENTER
6 MILES

Summary: Ride 11

0.0   From Red Lion Inn, go west on Route 102 for 0.4 miles.

0.4   Go straight at point where Route 102 goes right, cross Stockbridge golf course, go over bridge, bear right and up hill to Chesterwood sign, a total of 0.6 miles.

1.0   Go right at Chesterwood sign, uphill 0.7 miles.

1.7   Go left on Route 183 for 0.2 miles and second Chesterwood sign.

1.9   Go right for 0.1 miles, then left for 0.5 miles to Chesterwood.

2.5   From Chesterwood go back to Route 183, 0.6 miles.

3.1   Go left on Route 183 for 1.0 miles to intersection with Route 102.

4.1   Go right on Route 183 for 1.9 miles back to Red Lion Inn. (Or go left and look immediately right for Berkshire Garden Center.)

6.0   Total mileage.

Ride 12: Stockbridge-Lenox-South Lee-Tyringham-Monterey Workout

40.9 miles

This ride is ideal for bicyclists who enjoy a good day's workout over mostly rolling roads with no really formidable mountains. The ride starts at the Red Lion Inn, passes the Stockbridge Bowl, goes through Lenox, then heads south through mostly open agricultural country to Tyringham. After Tyringham it goes through a wooded area to Monterey, emerging in open country again on the way back to Stockbridge. If an early enough start is made a swim can be included at the Beartown State Forest, reached by a short sidetrip after going through Monterey. The major cultural attractions, and worth another stop, are the Tyringham Art Galleries and Gingerbread House, both in the same location.

From the Red Lion Inn the ride goes up Pine Street, directly across from the inn, and bears left for a two mile uphill over Prospect Hill, a way lined with estates on both sides and then the Stockbridge Bowl on the left. At the 4.8 mile mark, the trip goes right on Hawthorne Street in Lenox, marked by a triangle intersection, and continues climbing 2.2 miles to a stop sign and T intersection where it goes left for another 0.3 miles and emerges in front of the Curtis Hotel in the center of Lenox.

The ride then follows Route 7A south from the Curtis Hotel for 1.5 miles where it joins Route 7 and continues south on Route 7 for 2.5 miles where the High Lawn Farm appears on the left. The turnoff from Route 7, an oblique left, is 0.6 miles beyond the High Lawn Farm sign, an unmarked street called West Road. The road is followed through two stop signs, the first at 0.9 miles from Route 7 at an intersection with Devon Road, and the second 0.8 miles beyond the first at an intersection with Stockbridge Road.

The ride crosses the intersection where the name is changed to Church Street and follows it downhill for one mile to its intersection with Route 102 in South Lee. The route goes left on Route 102 for 0.1 miles where a sign points to the right to the Oak 'n Spruce resort. The right is taken and almost immediately the road crosses the Housatonic

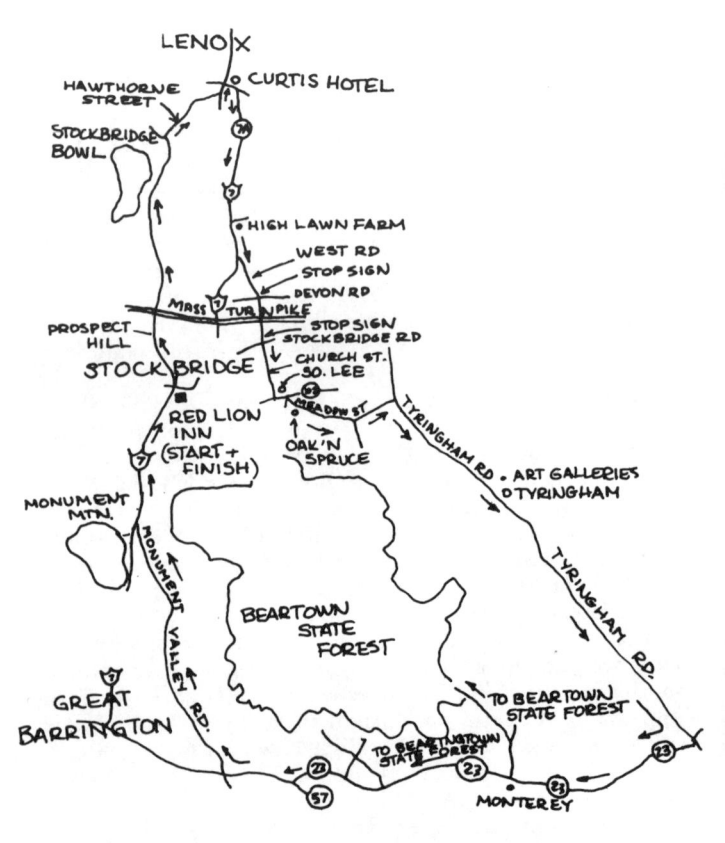

RIDE 12:
STOCKBRIDGE / LENOX / SOUTH LEE / TYRINGHAM / MONTEREY WORKOUT
40.9 MILES

River, then bears left on Meadow Street which goes by Oak 'n Spruce on the right. The ride continues over flat country with long views for 2.3 miles and the T intersection with the Tyringham Road where a right is taken.

That road heads southeast for 8.3 miles of beautiful views out over the Monument Mountain-Tyringham valley on the right until the intersection with Route 23. Along the way the Tyringham Art Galleries and Gingerbread House is on the left at 1.8 miles from the T intersection. At 3.7 miles beyond the gallery there's an almost mile-long climb before reaching Route 23.

A right on Route 23 takes the ride through mostly wooded areas heading towards Great Barrington. The town of Monterey, with a general store, is 3.7 miles along this section. Route 57 goes off to the left at the 8.0 mile mark, and Monument Valley Road, where the trip goes right, is at the 9.2 mile mark of mostly rolling terrain. Monument Valley Road affords a view of the valley from its other side for 4.7 miles to its intersection with Route 7 where the ride goes right for 2.7 downhill then flat miles to Stockbridge and the Red Lion Inn.

Summary of Ride 12

0.0   From Red Lion Inn, go across Main Street to Pine Street and bear left up Prospect Hill, a two mile climb. At 4.8 miles watch for Hawthorne Street turnoff.

4.8   Go right at Hawthorne Street for 2.2 miles to stop sign.

6.0   Go left at stop sign on Stockbridge Road for 0.3 miles.

6.3   Curtis Hotel. Go south on Route 7A for 1.5 miles to Route 7.

7.8   Go right on Route 7 for 2.5 miles, spotting High Lawn Farm sign on left, and then continuing for another 0.6 miles to oblique left.

Gingerbread House in Tyringham, and art gallery next door, are good places to visit during Ride 12.

10.9   Follow West Road, the oblique left, for 0.9 miles through first stop sign, for another 0.8 miles through second stop sign where West Street becomes Church Street, and for 1.0 miles downhill to intersection with Route 102.

13.6   Go left on Route 102 for 0.1 miles to sign pointing to Oak 'n Spruce.

13.7   Go right on road going to Oak 'n Spruce, bear left on Meadow Street and follow for 2.3 miles to T intersection with Tyringham Road.

16.0   Go right on Tyringham Road for 8.3 miles and intersection with Route 23.

24.3   Go right and follow Route 23 toward Great Barrington for 9.2 miles where Monument Valley Road comes in at right.

33.5   Go right on Monument Valley Road for 4.7 miles to intersection with Route 7.

38.2   Go right on Route 7 for 2.7 miles back to Red Lion Inn.

40.9   Total mileage.

Ride 13: Lenox Landscaper
31.3 miles

This ride is called the Lenox Landscaper because at one point or another it encompasses most of the views, landscape, residential and industrial, that make the Berkshires such a special place. The ride begins in Lenox, with its aristocratic heritage, proceeds along the Stockbridge Bowl past old estates, Tanglewood and Shadowbrook, skirts the northern border of Stockbridge and proceeds south through the mill town of Housatonic. From there it continues south a bit over flat country, but then goes west and north through the farmscapes surrounding the town of Alford and on to West Stockbridge. The final leg involves a climb over the Lenox Mountain and back to Lenox. Total mileage is 31.3, not excessively long as day rides go, but it should be noted that the final section is 2.2 miles over the Lenox Mountain, a part that can be avoided by going around the mountain for an additional 3.6 miles.

Begin the ride at the Curtis Hotel, following Route 183 south for 5.7 miles for a gradual rolling downhill that takes the cyclist past old estates, Tanglewood, Shadowbrook, the Stockbridge Bowl, and through the picturesque town of Interlaken. The ride crosses the intersection with Route 102 and continues south along Route 183 passing the Chesterwood turnoff at the 6.7 mile mark, and then following the Housatonic River and its rapids, to the gutted hulk of the Monument Mountain mill in Housatonic and the town itself. (Those interested in Victorian mill architecture might continue on Route 183 for 1.1 miles to see the Rising Paper Company mill, an imposing four story brick structure with two towers behind a row of tall spruces. The building is located at the end of an ample mill pond created by damming the Housatonic.)

Almost immediately after Route 183 passes the empty Monument Mountain mill it comes to a stop at Pleasant Street, where riders face the Pleasant Street market. Cross the intersecton, leaving the market on your immediate right and the railroad tracks on your left and proceed down Front Street which eventually becomes the Van Deusenville Road. The ride becomes flat. At 0.9 miles on this leg it goes over the first railroad crossing, at 1.4 miles it goes over a railroad

Near top of Lenox Mountain, vista opens out over Shadowbrook and Stockbridge Bowl. Plaque in foreground points to adjoining mountains.

crossing again, and at 1.9 miles it comes to a T intersection with Division Street, where there's a church on the left.

Go right at the intersection, cross Route 41 at one-tenth of a mile, and then ride for two miles to Division Road's intersection with the Alford Road, where you turn right. The ride then becomes a gradual uphill over rolling country for 1.4 miles to Alford, first marked by a town sign on the left. Go straight for another 0.2 miles and as you reach Alford's center, bear left at the Y, leaving the handsome New England church on the right. Then keep bearing right for another 0.3 miles, which will bring you out on West Road.

Proceed gradually uphill for 5.2 miles through exceptionally scenic countryside until its intersection with West Center Road, also a section offering unusually fine views. The value of panoramic views in this section of the Berkshires is reflected in the fact that about 60 percent of the land is reportedly owned by non-residents who have sought out quiet country places for retirement, vacations or investment. Take a left on West Center Road and follow it for 3.4 miles until its intersection with Route 102.

At Route 102 go right for 1.6 miles into West Stockbridge. As you approach the town you will notice an antique place called the Old Shaker Mill on your right, a concrete bridge over the Williams River is straight ahead, Main Street is a sharp right after the bridge and another street comes in from the left. Go straight, leaving a two-story frame house on your right, and if you've taken the right road out of this somewhat confusing intersection you'll see Mario's Garage on your left. There's also a faint sign at the intersection marked Lenox Road.

This is the beginning of a 2.2 mile climb over Lenox Mountain, which ends at a T intersection near the top where you make a right turn to head down the mountain for 1.5 bumpy miles to the road's intersection with Route 183. Go left on Route 183, past Tanglewood again, for 1.6 miles back to the Curtis Hotel.

Lenox Mountain can be avoided by staying on Route 102 heading towards Stockbridge to its intersection with Route 183 a distance of three miles. Go left on Route 183 for the 5.7 miles back to Lenox. Total mileage then would be 34.7 miles.

The ride can also start in Stockbridge at the Red Lion Inn by taking Route 102 west for 1.9 miles and its intersection with Route 183 where it turns left and heads towards Housatonic. Similarly, near the end at West Stockbridge, take Route 102 back to Stockbridge, a distance of five miles. The total mileage for the Stockbridge loop is 27.2 miles.

Summary: Ride 13

0.0   From Curtis Hotel, follow Route 183 south for 5.7 miles to intersection with Route 102.

5.7   Go straight through intersection, staying on Route 183 for 4.2 miles. (Turnoff to Chesterwood, studio of sculptor Daniel Chester French, is 1.0 miles from Route 102 intersection on Route 183).

9.9   Cross Pleasant Street in center of Housatonic, leaving Pleasant Street Market on right, railroad on left, and entering Front Street which later becomes Van Deusenville Road. First rail crossing is at 0.9 miles from Housatonic center, second rail crossing at 1.4 miles from Housatonic center. Follow this leg for total of 1.9 miles to T.

11.8   Go right at T. Church will be at left.

11.9   Cross Route 41 and continue on Division Street for 2.0 miles and intersection with Alford Road.

13.9   Go right for 1.6 miles to Alford, go left at Y, passing church on right and bearing right for 0.3 miles to West Road.

15.8   Follow West Road 5.2 miles to intersection with West Center Road.

21.0   Go left on West Center Road 3.4 miles to intersection with Route 102.

24.4   Go right on Route 102 for 1.6 miles to West Stockbridge.

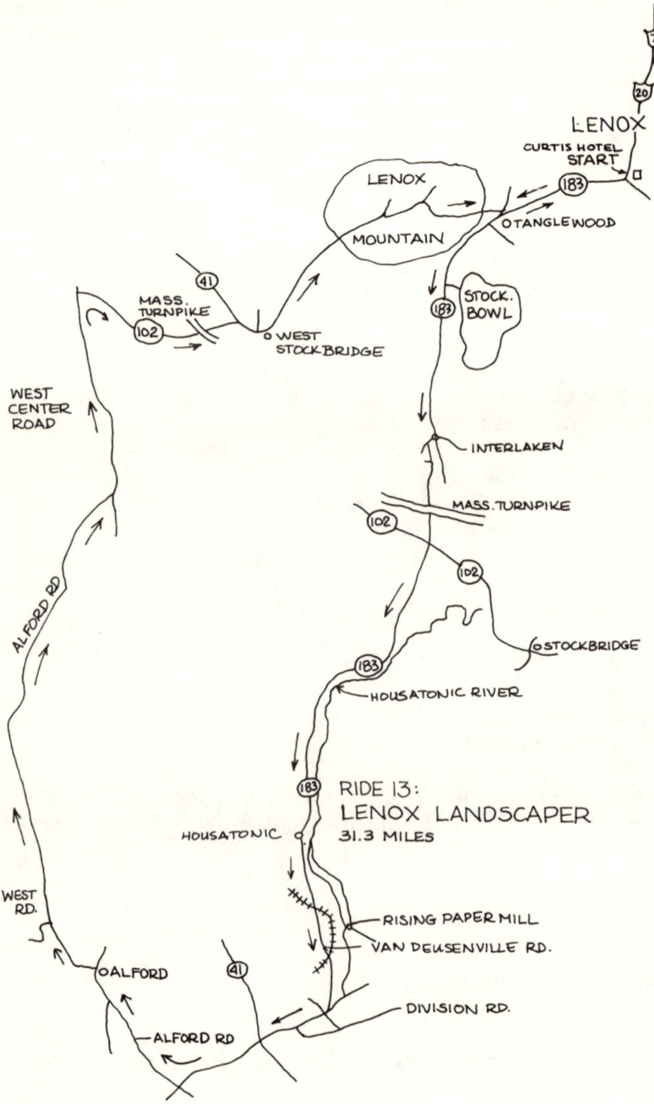
LENOX
CURTIS HOTEL
START
183
7
20
LENOX
MOUNTAIN
TANGLEWOOD
41
MASS. TURNPIKE
102
WEST STOCKBRIDGE
STOCK. BOWL
183
WEST CENTER ROAD
INTERLAKEN
MASS. TURNPIKE
102
102
ALFORD RD
STOCKBRIDGE
183
HOUSATONIC RIVER
183
RIDE 13:
LENOX LANDSCAPER
31.3 MILES
HOUSATONIC
WEST RD.
RISING PAPER MILL
VAN DEUSENVILLE RD.
ALFORD
41
DIVISION RD.
ALFORD RD

26.0   As you go into West Stockbridge, cross concrete bridge, and go straight for road leading to Lenox Mountain. Do not go right down Main Street, nor sharply left. Faint sign will point to "Lenox Road." You are right if Mario's Garage, an Exxon station, appears almost immediately at left. Climb hill for 2.2 miles.

28.2   Go right at T and head down mountain for 1.5 miles and intersection with Route 183.

29.7   Go left on Route 183 for 1.6 miles back to Curtis Hotel.

31.3   Total mileage.

If starting from Stockbridge:

0.0   From Red Lion Inn follow Route 102 west for 1.9 miles and intersection with Route 183, the 5.7 mile marker for trip from Lenox.

Then at West Stockbridge, 26.0 mile marker, take Route 102 back to Stockbridge for 5 miles.

27.2   Total mileage from Stockbridge.

If riders want to avoid Lenox Mountain near the end:

From 26.0 at left West Stockbridge, head south on Route 102 for 3.0 miles, go on Route 183 for 5.7 miles back to Lenox. 34.7 Total mileage.

Ride 14: Lenox Lollipop

5.9 miles

The ride is called the lollipop because it is an easy one to taste. Its colors are inviting, and its flavor, wrought from scenery ranging from Tanglewood to a duck pond, is sweet.

The ride begins at the Curtis Hotel and goes down Stockbridge Street for 0.3 miles and then goes right on Hawthorne Street for another 1.2 miles, all downhill, to a stop sign. Take a right at the stop sign and ride along a flat stretch with the Stockbridge Bowl on the left and the Tanglewood south entrance on the right for 0.7 miles until the road intersects with Route 183. Go right on Route 183 for 0.3 miles, and directly opposite Tanglewood's main entrance take a left on the 3.2 mile Under Mountain Road that goes up a gradual hill, passing a lovely duck pond on the left before the top. If you stop and aim a camera at the ducks they'll come at you, wondering why. Keep going, skirting the side of the valley past a beautiful horse farm, then follow the road as it makes a right back down into Lenox where it becomes Cliffwood Street and intersects with Main Street. Go right on Main Street for 0.2 miles back to the Curtis Hotel.

Summary: Ride 14

0.0   From Curtis Hotel, go down Stockbridge Street for 0.3 miles.

0.3   Go right on Hawthorne Street for 1.2 miles to stop sign.

1.5   Go right at stop sign for 0.7 miles. Stockbridge Bowl is on left, Tanglewood on right.

2.2   Go right on Route 183 for 0.3 miles and Tanglewood main entrance.

2.5   Go left on Under Mountain Road, just opposite Tanglewood main entrance. Road goes up and down gradual hill, eventually becomes Cliffwood Street when it

Ducks who live on Under Mountain Road, Lenox, come out to greet photographer.

gets back to center area of Lenox. Total distance is 3.2 miles.

5.7 At Main Street, Lenox, go right for 0.2 miles back to Curtis Hotel.

5.9 Total mileage.

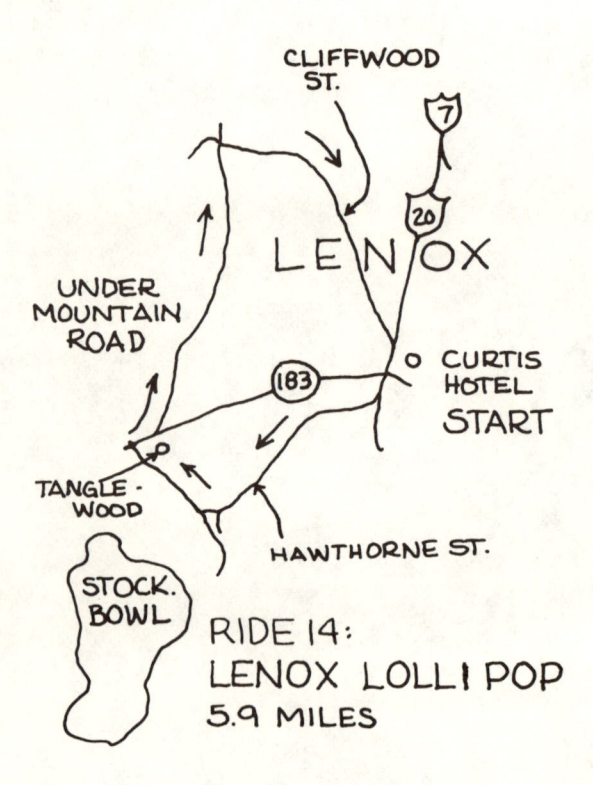

RIDE 14: LENOX LOLLIPOP
5.9 MILES

A Special Note for Rides 15 and 16

Rides 15 and 16 head north from Lenox. Ride 15 goes to the Hancock Shaker Village and back, a total of 26.3 miles; Ride 16 reaches Arrowhead, home of Herman Melville, as well as the Crane Museum in Dalton and the Stritch Studio in Hinsdale with its collection of iron sculpture.

Ride 15 is the more difficult, since it involves going over Lenox Mountain, a way that can be avoided by pedaling an extra 12.4 miles south, then north; or if riders forsake scenery, to follow Route 7 to Pittsfield through traffic, exhaust and gaudy signs. A third way is to take the beginning of Ride 16 to Pittsfield, go through Pittsfield and then follow Route 20 to the Hancock Shaker Village. Since the trade offs at getting around Lenox Mountain do not seem acceptable, the Lenox Mountain route for Ride 15 is recommended.

Ride 16 can be shortened by cutting out the leg to the Crane Museum or the leg to the Stritch Studio.

Ride 15: Lenox-Shaker Village
26.3 miles

The ride starts at the Curtis Hotel and proceeds south on Route 183 for 1.6 miles, past the main entrance to Tanglewood, to a road going off on the right, marked by a sign "To Rt. 41, Richmond — 5."

This is the road up over Lenox Mountain, a bumpy way for 1.5 miles to the top and then downhill for another 1.8 miles to its intersection with Swamp Road that goes left to West Stockbridge and right to Pittsfield. Cross the intersection and go straight on the Lenox Road, a flat section, for 1.2 miles until its intersection with Route 41, where the ride goes right. Make the turn and head 5.0 miles gradually uphill north to where Route 41 joins Route 20. The Hancock Village is at the left as the Route 20 intersection is approached. Entrance to the village is off Route 20.

To return to Lenox follow Route 20 towards Pittsfield for 3.6 miles, where at a traffic light Barker Road goes off to the right. Follow Barker Road for a mostly flat and scenic 6.7 miles to its intersection with the Lenox-Richmond Road, the same road travelled at the beginning of the ride. Take a left and go up and over the mountain for 3.3 bumpy miles, then a left on Route 183 for the 1.6 mile ride back to the Curtis Hotel.

If the mountain seems too much at this point, keep going straight on Swamp Road for three miles to West Stockbridge, three miles down Route 102 to its intersection with Route 183 and then 5.7 miles back to Lenox. Or, if you want to avoid the mountain in the beginning, take Route 183 out of Lenox all the way to Route 102, go right on Route 102 to West Stockbridge where you pick up Route 41 and the ride north to the Shaker Village.

Summary: Ride 15

0.0   From Curtis Hotel follow Route 183 south for 1.6 miles past Tanglewood's main entrance to Lenox Mountain Road where sign points to Route 41, Richmond — 5.

1.6   Go right on Lenox Mountain Road and up over Lenox Mountain to Swamp Road stop sign, 3.3 miles.

4.9   Cross Swamp Road, continuing straight for 1.2 miles on Lenox Road until intersection with Route 41.

6.1   Go right on Route 41 for 5.0 miles to Route 20 and the Hancock Shaker Village.

11.1   Go right on Route 20 for 3.6 miles to Barker Road that comes in from right and is marked by traffic light.

14.7   Go right on Barker Road for 6.7 miles and intersection with Lenox-Richmond Road, referred to above as Lenox Mountain Road and way previously travelled.

21.4   Go left and up over mountain for 3.3 miles to Route 183.

24.7   Go left on Route 183 for 1.6 miles back to Curtis Hotel.

26.3   Total mileage.

Round barn is one of characteristics of Hancock Shaker Village, near intersection of Routes 20 and 41, southwest of Pittsfield.

RIDE 15:
LENOX-SHAKER VILLAGE
26.3 MILES

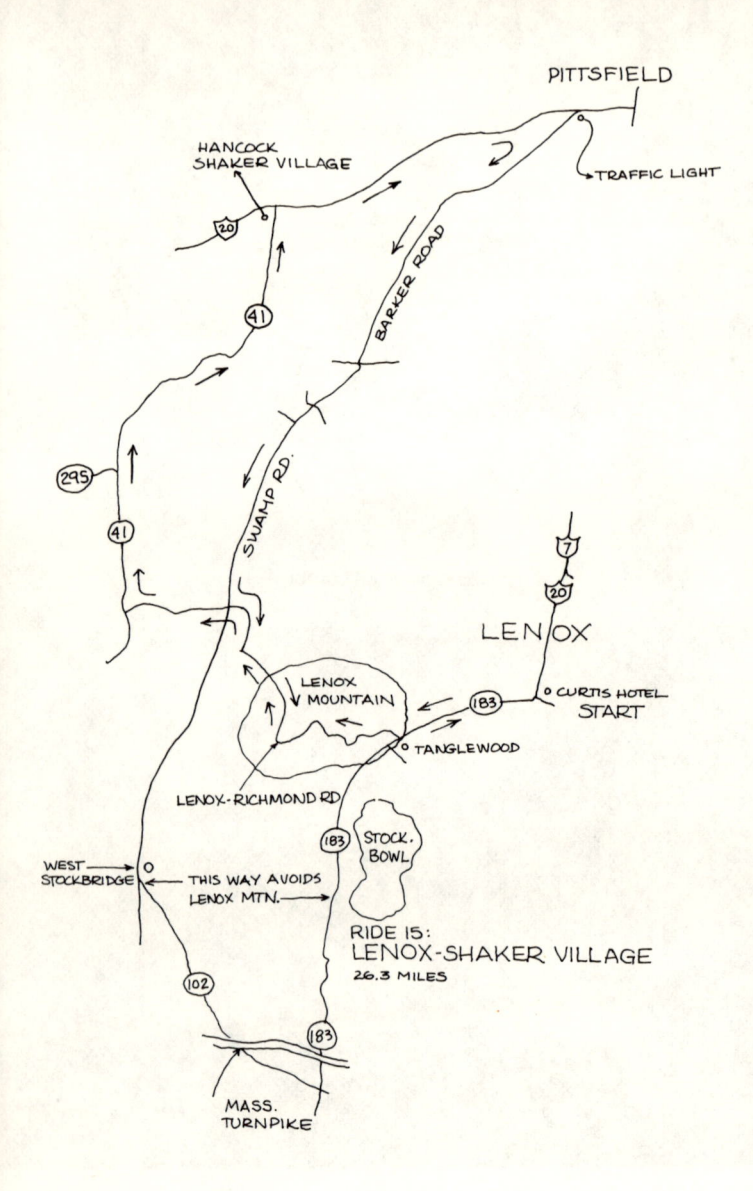

Lenox Mountain can be avoided at start by staying on Route 183 for 5.7 miles to intersection with Route 102, following Route 102 north to West Stockbridge for 3.0 miles where it joins Route 41.

On the way back, Barker Road becomes Swamp Road and is followed to West Stockbridge where Route 102 south may be picked up. Follow that for 3.0 miles, then go left on Route 183 for 5.7 miles back to Lenox.

Or shorten the whole trip and also avoid Lenox Mountain by taking Route 7 north to Pittsfield then left on Route 20. Expect heavy traffic.

Ride 16: Lenox-Arrowhead-Crane Museum and Stritch Sculpture Gardens
33.4 miles

This is mostly a flat ride to Pittsfield, passing Arrowhead where Herman Melville wrote Moby Dick. The ride proceeds through a residential area on a road where there's apt to be some heavy traffic during commuting periods, and then through a moderately congested area of Pittsfield to Dalton and the Crane Museum with its papermaking exhibits. The ride can then be extended to Hinsdale and the Stritch Sculpture Gardens with a return on a bumpy downhill to the Pittsfield line, and then back to Lenox on mostly secondary roads that are bumpy but not excessively so.

The ride begins at the Curtis Hotel and heads north on Route 7A for 0.4 miles where it goes right on Hubbard Street about halfway up the hill. In another 0.4 miles it crosses the double highway of Route 7 and then goes for another 0.8 miles to a T intersection with East Street.

Go left on East Street, and at 2.4 miles the Eastover resort is at the right, and possibly buffalo will be grazing in one of its fields, also on the right. Continue for another 2.6 miles until East Street meets Holmes Road and then head right on Holmes Road for 2.2 miles and its intersection with William Street, marked by an overhead blinker light. Along Holmes Road on the left is Arrowhead, the home of Herman Melville and the headquarters for the Berkshire County Historical Society.

Go right on William Street, being thankful for its wide shoulders, and ride 2.0 miles to Division Road, where you make a left for 1.7 miles to a stop sign at its intersection with South Street. Go right on South Street for 1.6 miles and up a final small hill to its intersection with Routes 8 and 9 and the Crane Museum.

At the Crane Museum, head east on Routes 8 and 9, following Route 8, after it parts from Route 9, into Hinsdale, 4.9 miles, where the ride goes left on Route 143 for an 0.8 mile climb to the Stritch Sculpture Gardens. Coming back onto Route 8, continue for another 3.2 miles to the Pittsfield Road, the second right after the railroad bridge, a turn that goes back on itself sharply. Follow the road, which is mostly bumpy and downhill, for 4.8 miles back to Division Road and William Street.

Take William Street towards Pittsfield for 1.4 miles, going left on the East New Lenox Road for three miles over mostly bumpy surfaces. When it comes to a stop sign go right for 1.1 miles to a second stop sign, where you go left, again on East Street, for 2.5 miles back to Hubbard Street, where you go right for 1.6 miles back to Main Street in Lenox and the Curtis Hotel.

The ride can be shortened by 12.9 miles by taking out the loop to the Stritch Museum. And for an even shorter ride that goes to Arrowhead but not the other two attractions, go to William Street in Pittsfield and head right for 0.6 miles to the East New Lenox Road, where you take another right, to head back to Lenox. This makes a total distance of 14.4 miles.

Summary: Ride 16

0.0   From Curtis Hotel, follow Route 7A north for 0.4 miles to Hubbard Street.

0.4   Go right on Hubbard Street for 0.4 miles, cross Route 7, and go another 0.8 miles to T intersection at East Street.

1.6   Go left on East Street for 3.4 miles to Holmes Road, Pittsfield.

5.0   Follow Holmes Road north to William Street for 2.2 miles. Arrowhead is on left.

6.2   Go right on William Street for 2.0 miles to Division Road.

8.2   Go left on Division Road for 1.7 miles to South Street stop sign.

9.9   Go right on South Street 1.6 miles to intersection of Routes 8 and 9 and Crane Museum.

11.5   Follow Routes 8 and 9, then Route 8 east and south for 4.9 miles to Route 143.

16.4 Go left on Route 143 for 0.8 miles to Stritch Sculpture Gardens.

17.2 Head back down to Route 8, 0.8 miles.

18.0 Go left on Route 8 for 3.2 miles to Pittsfield Road.

21.2 Go sharply right on Pittsfield Road for 4.8 miles back to Division Road and William Street.

26.0 Follow William Street to East New Lenox Road, 1.4 miles.

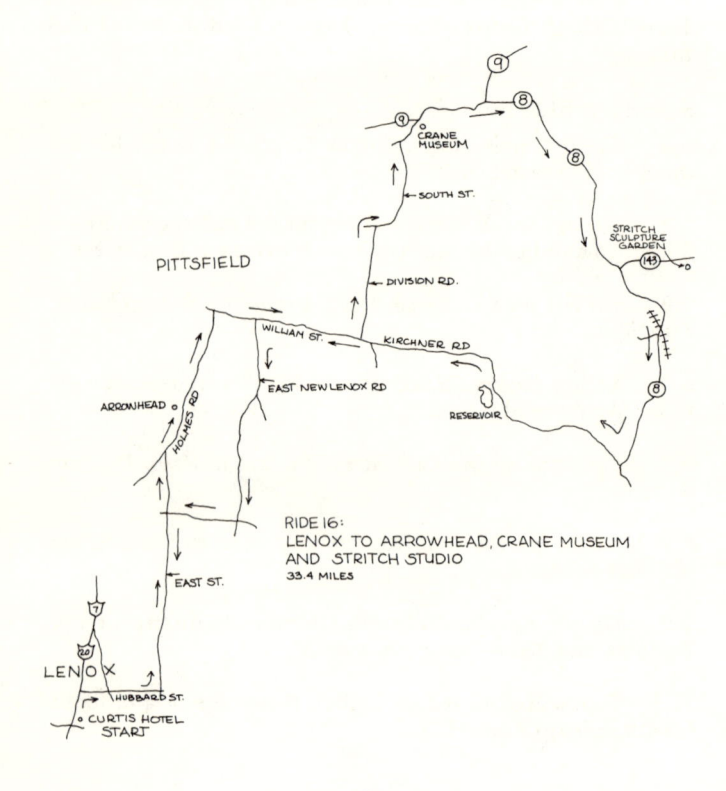

RIDE 16:
LENOX TO ARROWHEAD, CRANE MUSEUM AND STRITCH STUDIO
33.4 MILES

27.4 Go left on East New Lenox Road for 3.0 miles to stop sign.

30.4 Go right at stop sign for 1.1 miles to second stop sign, East Street.

31.5 Go left on East Street for 2.5 miles to Hubbard Street.

34.0 Go right on Hubbard Street, then left on Route 7A for 1.6 miles back to Curtis Hotel.

35.6 Total mileage.

Route can be shortened by 12.9 miles by turning around at Crane Museum and not taking extra Route 8 loop. It can also be shortened by making right on William Street and going for 0.6 miles to East New Lenox Road and then right, picking up above trip at 27.4 mile mark. This would make a total of 14.4 miles.

Pittsfield has two lakes, Onota and Pontoosuc. Ride 18 goes around Onota, but if bicyclists want to cope with heavier traffic on Rt. 7, the way will lend to Pontoosuc, whose surface is seen through pines near entrance to recreation facility.

Chapter 4:
Pittsfield: Berkshire's Urban Place

Bicycle tourists do not come to Berkshire County to bicycle in Pittsfield, the county seat, its largest city, and the financial and retail hub of central Berkshire. Nonetheless, because of the geography, bicyclists going from south to north or north to south must go through Pittsfield and recommended through routes are suggested in the section entitled North-South Link.

The city itself, however, has several interesting attractions that make it easy to spend a day. North Street, the main shopping area, has a variety of stores as well as movie theaters and Park Square, ringed by historic buildings, is the original village square with the streets named North, South, East and West going their various directions to form the spines of the city's layout.

The Berkshire Museum on South Street is certainly worth a visit and so is Arrowhead, the home of Herman Melville on Holmes Road. Swimmers will enjoy the city's recreation facilities on Pontoosuc Lake and bicyclists interested in comfort and civilized surroundings should investigate the Hilton Inn.

Pittsfield also offers South Mountain Concerts on Routes 7 and 20, one mile south of the city. Performances are on Saturday afternoons in June, July and August, and Sundays in September and October. A complex of estate, concert hall and musicians' cottages, South Mountain Concerts was founded in 1918 for chamber music, still its major offering.

The largest industry in Pittsfield (and the county), is General Electric, which makes transformers and also works on military contracts. General Electric was established in Pittsfield in 1903 when it bought the Stanley Electric Co., founded by the man who had discovered alternating current as a means of transmitting electricity.

Like so many of its urban counterparts throughout the United States the story of Pittsfield (named in 1761 for Prime Minister William Pitt) is one of agriculture, industry, decline and recovery. In 1979 that recovery was taking the form of a massive downtown redevelopment project being planned for the western side of North Street.

The major tourist attraction in Pittsfield, and certainly a stop recommended for everyone with an interest in the county, is the Berkshire Museum on South Street, only a minute or so away from Park Square by foot. Small enough to tour in about an hour, the museum has a local history room in its basement as well as other offerings of both regional and general interest. The facility is open Tuesday through Saturday from 10 a.m. to 5 p.m., and Sundays from 2 to 5 p.m. Admission is free.

Three other chief tourist attractions in and around Pittsfield have already been described in the introduction to Chapter 2. They are Arrowhead on Holmes Road, the home of Herman Melville, Stritch Sculpture Gardens in Hinsdale and the Crane Museum in Dalton.

The latter two may be reached by taking Ride 17. Arrowhead may be reached by following the first part of Ride 17, East Street and Elm Street, and then making a right on Holmes from Elm, following Holmes to Arrowhead. The round trip distance from Park Square is about five miles.

Ride 17: Park Square to Dalton and Hinsdale

22.8 miles

This is a fairly easy ride that is mostly flat, yet has two major points of interest, the Crane Museum in Dalton and the Stritch Sculpture Gardens in Hinsdale. Since going to the Stritch gardens involves an extra 12.9 mile loop, the ride can be shortened, although riders will miss seeing some unusual sculpture and meeting the jovial creator of these works of art.

The ride starts at Park Square and heads east on East Street for 0.4 miles and then at the third set of lights bears right on Elm Street, where it continues for 1.9 miles to William Street. All of this portion is through city traffic. William Street, however, has a nice wide shoulder and by this time the traffic has thinned. Bear left on William Street, following it for 1.0 mile to Division Road, the boundary between Pittsfield and Dalton, where the ride goes left.

Park Square, ringed by historic buildings, is the original village green of Pittsfield, the county seat.

Follow Division Road for 1.7 miles to a stop sign on South Street, turn right and go 1.6 miles to its intersection with Routes 8 and 9 and the Crane Museum.

Extending the trip to visit the Stritch Gardens means following Routes 8 and 9 east, and then bearing right on Route 8 for 3.0 miles until Route 143, which comes in from the left at Hinsdale. Turn left on Route 143 and climb the hill for 0.8 miles until you reach the Stritch Sculpture Gardens on your right.

To return, head back down the hill, go left on Route 8 for 5.1 miles to the Pittsfield Road, which is the second right after the railroad bridge and which requires almost a U-Turn to negotiate. The pavement unfortunately turns bumpy, but it is downhill, skirting October Mountain State Forest for 4.8 miles back to Division Road, then William Street, Elm Street, East Street and Park Square, the way the ride began.

The stretch of ride between Hinsdale and Pittsfield Road, and then along Pittsfield Road back to Division Road, is sparsely populated and therefore a bit lonely.

Summary: Ride 17

0.0   Start at Park Square and head east on East Street for 0.4 miles; at third set of lights go right on Elm Street.

0.4   Follow Elm Street (at 1.0 miles go right at Holmes Road if going to Arrowhead or Lenox) to William Street, 1.9 miles.

2.3   Bear left on William Street and go 1.0 miles to Division Road.

3.3   Go left on Division Road for 1.7 miles to South Street stop sign.

5.0   Go right on South Street 1.6 miles to intersection with Routes 8 and 9 and Crane Museum.

6.6   Go right on Routes 8 and 9, bear right on Route 8, 8.1 miles to Pittsfield Road. (If going to Stritch Sculpture

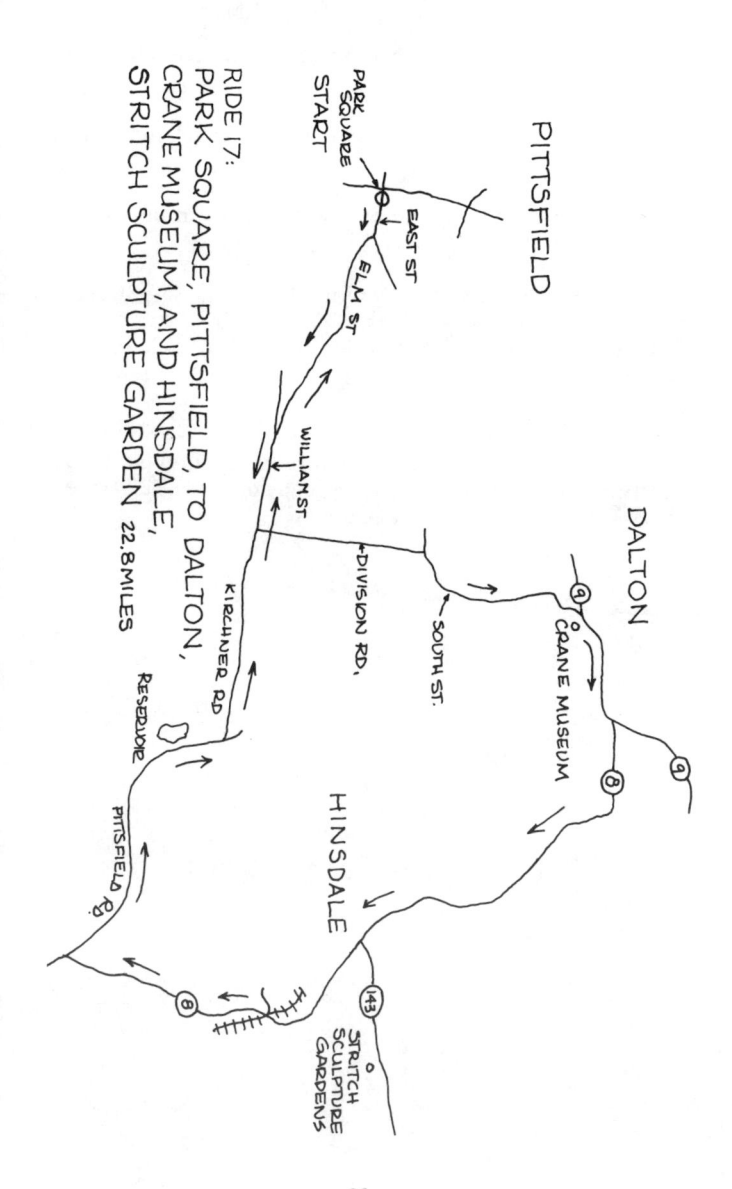

PITTSFIELD

RIDE 17:
PARK SQUARE, PITTSFIELD, TO DALTON,
CRANE MUSEUM, AND HINSDALE,
STRITCH SCULPTURE GARDEN 22.8 MILES

Gardens, take left on Route 143 at Hinsdale and climb hill for 0.8 miles.)

14.7 Go right on Pittsfield Road, 4.8 milesback to Division Road and William Street.

19.5 Go straight on William Street for 1 mile to Elm Street.

20.5 Bear right on Elm Street for 1.9 miles to East Street.

22.4 Go left on East Street for 0.4 miles back to Park Square.

22.8 Total mileage.

This trip can be shortened by turning around at Crane Museum and not taking Route 8 loop for extra 12.9 miles. This would make total mileage 9.9 miles.

Ride 18: Pittsfield Onota Lake Ride Around

9.7 miles

This is also a fairly flat ride that offers views of Lake Onota and, if you don't mind a gradual climb, picnicking at Pittsfield State Forest. The ride starts at Park Square and follows West Street for 0.5 miles where it goes left at a stop sign and follows the directional sign to Berkshire Community College. At 2.7 miles from Park Square just before the college (which makes a nice optional short side trip), turn right on Churchill Street and follow it straight. The turnoff to the state forest is at 4.5 miles on Churchill Street and the entrance is another 0.7 miles after a gradual uphill. At 5.1 miles on Churchill Street, turn right on Dan Casey Memorial Drive, a causeway that goes over the north section of Onota Lake, for 0.5 miles.

At the end of the causeway, go right on Peck's Road for 0.8 miles, then right on Valentine Road and up a hill for 1.9 miles to the intersection with West Street that the ride passed in its beginning part. Go left at the stop light on West Street, follow it for 0.9 miles and then right as the business district comes into view, for 0.5 miles back to Park Square.

The ride can be extended for 1.5 miles by going straight on Churchill Street to Hancock Road, then right for a bumpy 0.4 miles to Balance Rock Road in Lanesboro. Turn right on Balance Rock, which becomes Peck's Road at the boundary. Or, if you don't mind dirt roads, extend it for another 2.5 miles by following Churchill Street all the way to its end, a 1.0 mile leg, then turn right on Potter Mountain Road going downhill to Balance Rock Road, where you take another right to finish the trip.

Summary: Ride 18

0.0   Start at Park Square and head west on West Street.

0.5   Go left at stop sign, following sign to BCC for 2.2 miles.

2.7   At Churchill Street go right (at 1.5 miles turnoff for Pittsfield State Forest, follow that road for 0.7 miles to entrance). Follow Churchill Road for 2.4 miles.

RIDE 18:
PITTSFIELD - ONOTA
RIDE AROUND

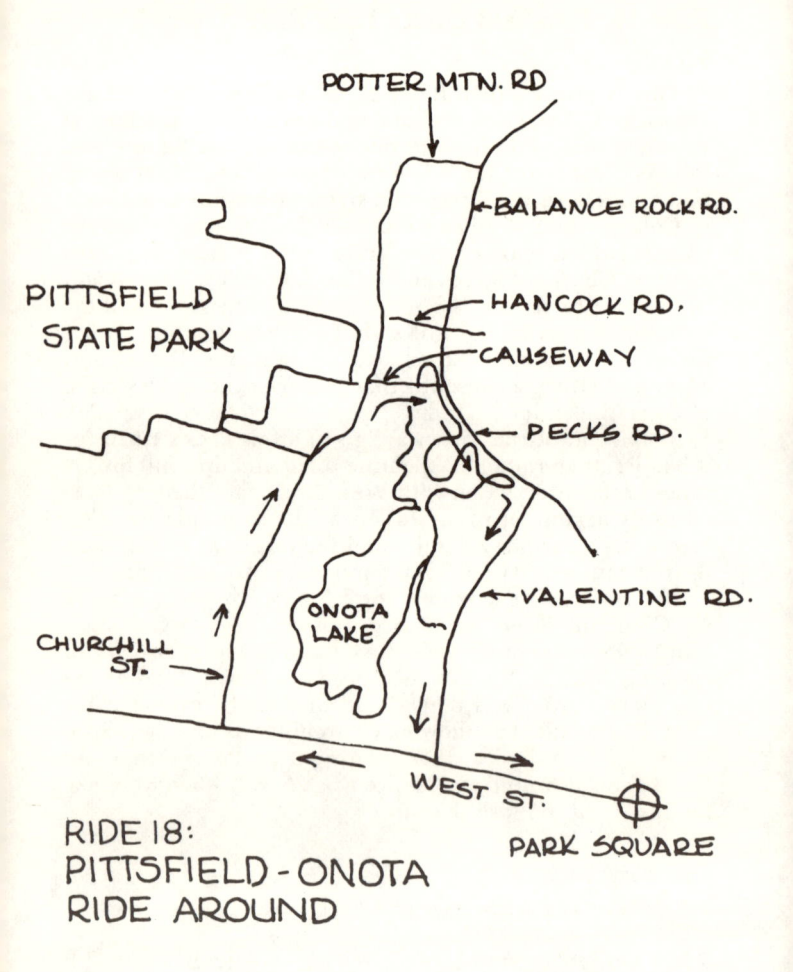

5.1 Go right on Dan Casey Memorial Drive and follow for 0.5 miles.

5.6 Go right on Peck's Road for 0.8 miles.

6.4 Go right on Valentine Road and uphill for 1.9 miles.

8.3 Go left at stop light on West Street for 0.9 miles, and go right by Western Mass Electric Company and Salvation Army.

9.2 Go right for 0.5 miles back to Park Square.

9.7 Total mileage.

Can be extended 1.5 miles:
At 5.1 miles keep going straight on Churchill Street to Hancock Road, 0.5 miles. Go right on Hancock Road for 0.4 miles and then right on Balance Rock Road for 0.6 miles, where it joins the first trip at the 5.6 mile mark.

Can be extended for another 2.5 miles:
Keep going on Churchill Street past Hancock Road where it turns to dirt road for 1.0 miles, then right on Potter Mountain Road for 0.4 miles, then right on Balance Rock for 1.1 miles.

Ride 19: North-South Link

30.2 miles

Although Pittsfield is not at the geographic center of Berkshire County, psychologically it seems to be because it is the county's largest populated area with the most complex maze of streets. There is really no good way for a bicyclist to go from north county to south county without dealing with Pittsfield. Motorists deal with it by using Routes 7 or 8 on its north, Route 9 on its east, Route 20 on its west and Route 7 on its south, the main traffic arteries. To avoid the main routes, we've worked out a somewhat complex, but scenic, route from the north to the south, a route that is used in part for the Great Josh Billings Runaground race each fall. The ride, from its beginning at the Sheraton Inn in North Adams to its connection with Route 41 in Pittsfield, is 30.2 miles long with both up and downhills.

If done from the north, the ride starts at the Sheraton in North Adams and heads south for 0.3 miles on American Legion Drive, past The Transcript, and then turns right on Ashland Street for 1.2 miles where it again bears right at a gasoline station and goes for another 1.2 miles, leaving a cemetery on its right, to the intersection with East Road, where there's a small traffic island and the McCann Regional Vocational School off to the right.

Stay on East Road for 5.7 miles until its intersection with Route 116. The ride is a gradual uphill climb that affords sweeping views of Mount Greylock off to the right. The first hill comes almost immediately, is about two miles long, but not terribly steep, with stretches of flat. The ride evens out a bit and goes by the birthplace of Susan B. Anthony on the left at the 6.3 mile mark, the intersection of East and Walling Roads. At the 7.1 mile mark a short (0.4 miles) steep hill that may require walking begins, but the top offers a beautiful view to the east and then about a four-mile gradual downhill.

At the intersection of Route 116 go right for 0.3 miles and then left on Wells Road, continuing the downhill for 3.5 miles into the town of Cheshire where you make a right on its Main Street, following it for 0.5 miles until its intersection with Route 8.

Turn left on Route 8, a main road, for 0.3 miles, then

right on the Lanesboro Road, for 4.3 miles, a bit of a climb that goes on the high side of Hoosac Lake. Lanesboro Road ends with a stop sign at a T intersection where the ride goes right, up a short hill, and then down, for a total of 0.6 miles to Lanesboro on Route 7.

Go left on Route 7, heading south, for 1.2 miles and then turn right on Bull Hill Road for 0.9 miles, going up the hill and then right on Balance Rock Road that eventually becomes Peck's Road in Pittsfield for a total of 3.5 miles.

Watch for Valentine Road, a fairly new way with good pavement and shoulders and go right, following it for 1.8 miles over a hill in the beginning. Go left at the stop light on West Street and either follow West Street all the way in to downtown Pittsfield, or go right on Mirriam Street after 0.7 miles, and then take another right on Route 20, for 0.1 miles to Barker Road, or 3.6 miles to the intersection with Route 41. Both Barker and Route 41 go to West Stockbridge. There's a cutoff from Barker to Lenox over the Lenox Mountain. Route 41 is a gradual downhill to West Stockbridge, and Barker Road is mostly flat.

Summary: Ride 19

0.0   Sheraton Inn in North Adams, head out on American Legion Drive.

0.3   Go right on Ashland Street for 1.2 miles, bearing right at Getty station. Go another 1.2 miles to East Road intersection.

2.7   Go left on East Road and continue 5.7 miles to intersection with Route 116.

8.4   Go right at Route 116 for 0.3 miles.

8.7   Left on Wells Road for 3.5 miles.

12.2   Right on Main Street, Cheshire, for 0.5 miles until intersection with Route 8.

12.7   Go left on Route 8 for 0.3 miles.

**RIDE 19:
NORTH - SOUTH LINK
30.2 MILES**

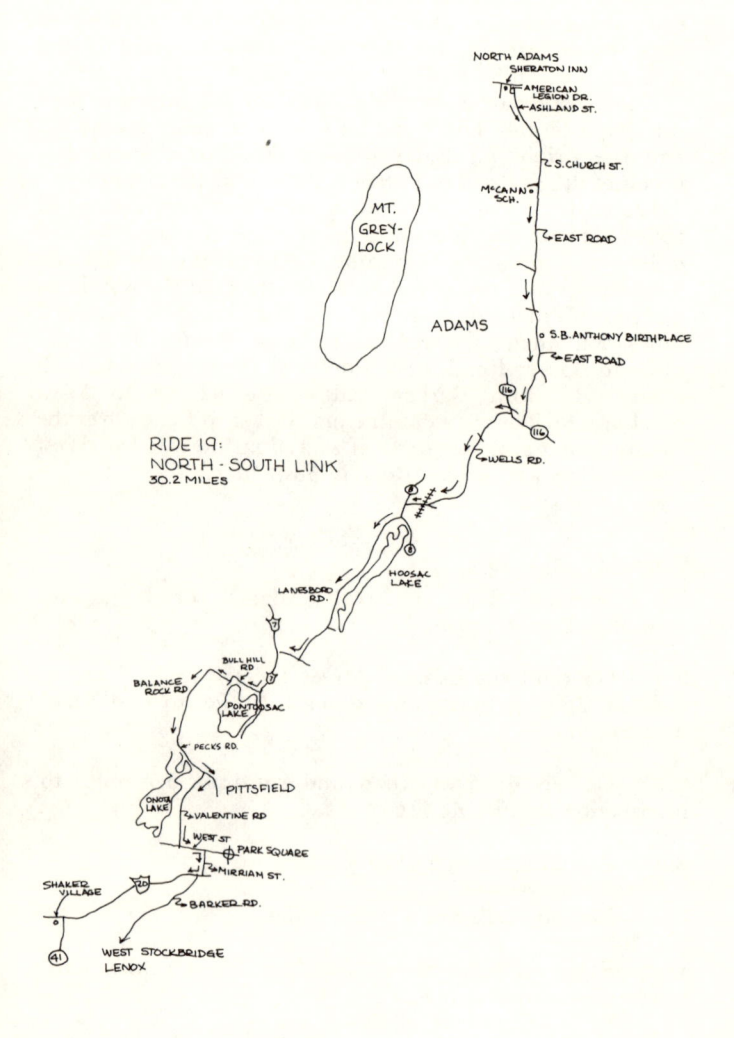

13.0 Go right on Lanesboro Road for 4.3 miles.

17.3 Go right at stop sign at T, 0.3 mile climb to top of hill then long downhill to Route 7, total 0.6 miles.

17.9 Left on Route 7 for 1.2 miles heading south to Bull Hill Road.

19.1 Bull Hill Road go right for 0.9 miles.

20.0 Go right on Balance Rock Road for 1.7 miles. The pavement changes and becomes Peck's Road. Continue for total 3.5 miles.

23.5 Go right on Valentine Road for 1.8 miles.

25.3 Go left at stop light on West Street for 0.7 miles.

26.0 Right on Mirriam Street for 0.5 miles.

26.5 Right on Route 20 for 0.1 miles to Barker Road.

26.6 Barker Road (keep going straight for 3.6 miles for intersection with Route 41.)

30.2 Route 41 and total mileage.

High on Mount Greylock.

Chapter 5:
Mount Greylock: Head for the Sky

Described by one writer as the "high lord of the Berkshires" Mount Greylock dominates the northern part of the county and, on a clear day, most of the rest of the county too, since it looks down on every other mountain in the Berkshires, including Mount Everett way to the south.

The name probably stems from the mountain's often gray appearance, caused by ice crystallizing on the trees near the top on cold days, literally giving the mountain a "gray look." The mountain stands by itself, 3,491 feet high, between two other mountain ranges, the Taconic on the west that separates Massachusetts from New York, and the Hoosac on the right, which walls off northern Berkshire County from the rest of Massachusetts. To the north of Mount Greylock are the Green Mountains of Vermont, and to the south, the smaller mountains of the Berkshires. Immediately at its base, almost underneath the mountain as you ride the final mile to the summit, lies the town of Adams. As a result of Mt. Greylock, the terrain of northern Berkshire is either valley or mountain. There's very little of the open rolling country found in the southern part of the county.

In many respects Mount Greylock provides the visual reward for bicycle touring in northern Berkshire because each trip offers different, and mostly spectacular, views of this majestic mountain.

But climbing Mount Greylock on a bicycle is a reward in itself, not only because of the sense of real accomplishment it provides, but also because the trip can be made into a nice leisurely two-day camping expedition, perfect for a weekend, that can boast views among the finest in all of New England.

Michael H. Farny, author of "New England Over the Handlebars", a work published in 1975, had this to say about Mount Greylock:

"For cyclists who want a wonderful mountain experience, Greylock offers the finest there is. At 3,491 feet, Greylock is

photograph by Christopher Gillooly

the highest mountain in Massachusetts. Cadillac Mountain on Mount Desert may be more exposed, Smugglers Notch may be steeper, and Mt. Washington may be far higher, but the sixteen-mile route up and over Mt. Greylock is the loveliest in New England."

The trip is a good one because the roads to the summit are smooth and well-paved. There's also no-frills lodging at the summit, or for those who prefer to rough it, a tent campsite near the summit and one Adirondack three-sided shelter a mile or so beyond if more isolation is preferred.

Rockwell Road approaches the summit from Lanesboro and Notch Road from North Adams, an arrangement that means the trip can be done as a loop from either North Adams, Adams, Williamstown or Pittsfield, or as an up and over from the south or north. However, since Rockwell Road is the more gradual approach, it is recommended for the ascent with the descent into North Adams. The Rockwell Road approach also makes it easier for camping since it provides access to the tent site on Stony Ledge. If the trip is made from North Adams the climb is a bit steeper, especially in the beginning, and will probably require some walking.

In any event, the trip should not be undertaken unless bicyclists are in reasonably good shape. If some are and some aren't, those who aren't can drive to the top by car for a rendezvous with the more conditioned bikers.

Rides 20A, 20B, 20C, 20D, 20E:
Five Ways to the Visitor's Center

Assuming that riders will follow the recommendation to make the trip up Mount Greylock from the Lanesboro side, the location of the visitor's center, there are five different loops that are possible: one from Pittsfield, one from Williamstown, two from North Adams and one from Adams. Wherever the ride originates, the actual climb begins at the visitor's center, goes to the summit, and then ends on the North Adams side.

Accordingly, five routes to the visitor's center are described as rides 20A through 20E. Ride 21 is the ride to the top, then down the other side, a distance of 17.7 miles from the visitor's center to Route 2, North Adams.

Ride 20A: Pittsfield to Visitor's Center
12.1 miles

The ride begins at Park Square and follows West Street for 0.5 miles where it goes left at a stop sign, in the direction indicated by a sign pointing to Berkshire Community College. Follow West Street for another 0.9 miles to its intersection with Valentine Road where there's a stop light. Go right on Valentine Road for 1.8 miles, going up, then down a hill, turn left on Peck's Road, following it for 1.8 miles to the Pittsfield-Lanesboro line where it becomes Balance Rock Road. Take Balance Rock Road for 1.7 miles, then go left on Bull Hill Road for 0.9 miles to Route 7, where the ride goes left and heads north for 2.6 miles.

At the 10.2 mark from Park Square, a sign will point to the Greylock Reservation indicating a right on North Main Street, which shortly becomes Quarry Road where the ride bears right for 1.2 miles to Rockwell Road. Go left on Rockwell Road for 0.7 miles to the visitor's center, which will be on your right.

Ride 20B: Williamstown to Visitor's Center
15.8 miles

From Field Park in front of the Williams Inn head south on Route 7, a wide, smoothly paved road, for 13.9 miles and the sign pointing to the Greylock Reservation. Make a left, as indicated by the sign, onto North Main Street, then bear right on Quarry Road for a total of 1.2 miles to Rockwell Road. Go left on Rockwell Road for 0.7 miles to the visitor's center. The stretch from Williamstown is mostly flat.

Ride 20C: North Adams to Visitor's Center, westerly route
21.9 miles

The ride starts at the Sheraton Inn and heads up West Main Street, with City Hall on the left and the Mohawk Center on the right, for 0.2 miles until West Main intersects with Route 2. Go left to merge into Route 2, following it for 0.1 miles to Notch Road, the North Adams approach to Mount Greylock. Keep going for another 0.3 miles on Route 2 then turn right at Roberts Drive for 0.2 miles where it

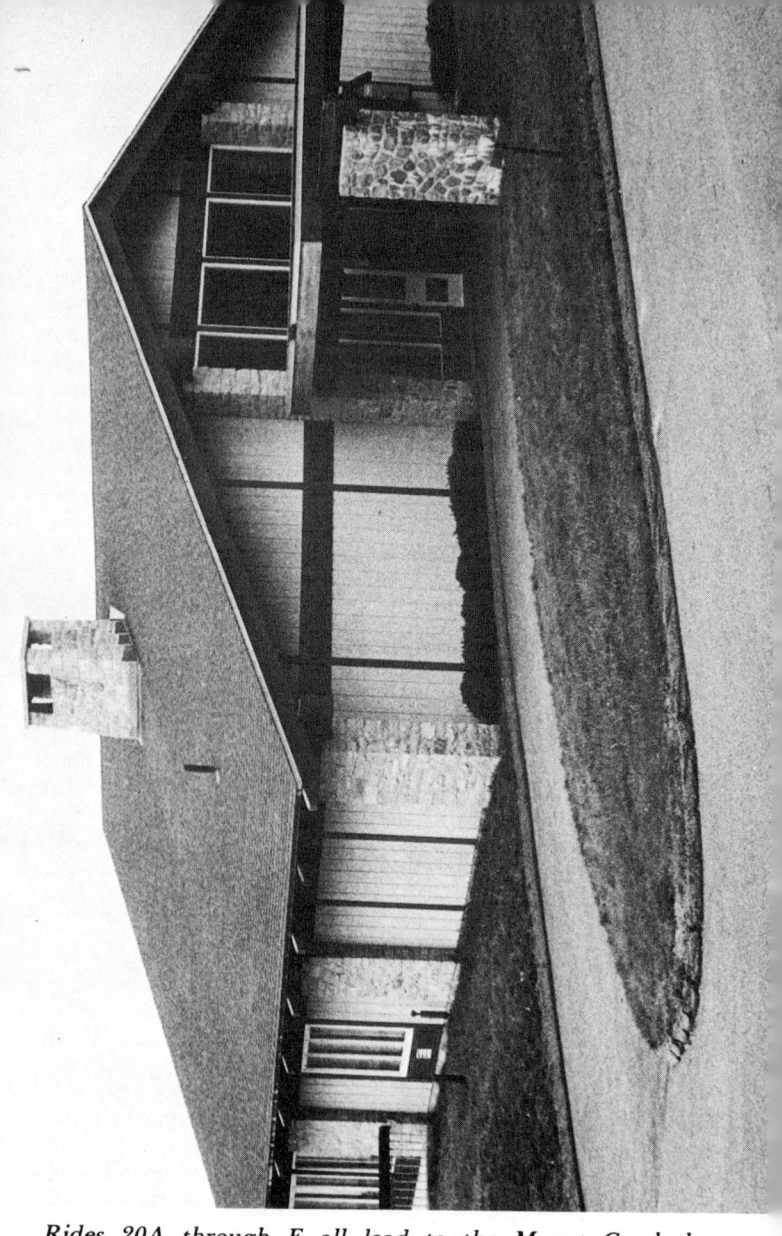

Rides 20A through E all lead to the Mount Greylock Visitor's Center that contains a relief model of the mountain and other information.

merges with Massachusetts Avenue. Follow the direction of the merge (left) for 3.1 miles until Cole Avenue intersects in Williamstown. Go left on Cole Avenue , over the railroad bridge and the Hoosac River for 0.7 miles to Route 2, then right on Route 2 for 0.1 miles and left on Water Street, which is marked as Route 43.

Follow Water Street, which becomes Green River Road, for 4.8 miles, enjoying one of the prettier rides in northern Berkshire with the river on your left and a picnic park, Mount Hope, 2.5 miles from the turnoff onto Route 43. This total leg is 4.8 miles and it leads to Route 7 at Steele's Corners where you go left, and south for 9.6 miles to the sign indicating the Mount Greylock Reservation. Go left on North Main Street, bear right on Quarry Road for a total of 1.2 miles to Rockwell Road where the ride turns left for 0.7 miles to the visitor's center. This approach is mostly flat.

Ride 20D: North Adams to Visitor's Center, easterly route

21.2 miles

The ride begins at the Sheraton Inn and heads south on American Legion Drive, past The Transcript for 0.3 miles, until it intersects with Ashland Street. Go right on Ashland Street, following it for 1.2 miles, bear right at the Getty station and keep going for another 1.2 miles to the East Road intersection, marked by a small traffic island and the McCann Regional Vocational School off to the right.

Bear left on East Road and continue 5.7 miles to its intersection with Route 116. Almost immediately a gradual climb will begin, with some flat stages. A bit farther along there will be a short, steep climb. The ride is marked by sweeping views of Mount Greylock on the right, Susan B. Anthony's birthplace at the intersection of East and Walling Roads, and near the end, a panoramic view of rolling country to the east.

Go right on Route 116, and then downhill for 0.3 miles, making a left on Wells Road for more downhill, this time 3.5 miles, until it merges with Main Street, Cheshire. Follow it for 0.5 miles until its intersection with Route 8.

Turn left on Route 8 for 0.3 miles, then right on Lanesboro Road for 4.3 miles, a gradual but rolling climb on the high side of Hoosac Lake. The road will end at a T intersection where the ride goes right, climbs 0.3 miles to the top of a hill, then 0.6 miles downhill to Route 7. Turn right on Route 7 and head north for 1.4 miles to the sign for the Mount Greylock Reservation. Go right on North Main Street, bear right on Quarry Road for 1.2 miles to Rockwell Road and turn left for 0.7 miles to the visitor's center.

Ride 20E: Adams to Visitor's Center

13.1 miles

The ride starts at McKinley Square on Park Street and climbs up Maple Street for 0.4 miles until it intersects with West Road. Turn left on West Road, which becomes the Fred Mason Road in Cheshire, travelling a total of 3.5 miles to its intersection with Route 8. On your right Mount Greylock will seem almost above you, you are so close to its lower slopes.

At Route 8 head south for 1.0 miles, through the town of Cheshire to Lanesboro Road, where the ride turns right and climbs the high side of Hoosac Lake for 4.3 gradually uphill rolling miles. Go right at the T intersection, climb the hill for 0.3 miles, then descend for 0.6 miles into Lanesboro and Route 7. Go right on Route 7, heading north for 1.4 miles to the sign marking the Greylock Reservation. Turn right on North Main Street, then bear right on Quarry Road for 1.2 miles to Rockwell Road. Take a left on Rockwell Road for 0.7 miles to the visitor's center.

Summary: Rides 20A-E

Mt. Greylock ride starts at visitor's center in Lanesboro accessible from Pittsfield, North Adams, or Williamstown. It can also be done the other way but the more gradual climb is from Lanesboro up, with five loops possible: one from Pittsfield, one from Williamstown, two from North Adams, one from Adams.

Ride 20A: Pittsfield to Visitor's Center

0.0   Park Square, follow West Street west for 0.5 miles.

0.5   Go left at stop sign, follow sign to Berkshire Community College for 0.9 miles to Valentine Road stoplight.

1.4   Go right on Valentine Road for 1.8 miles.

3.2   Go left on Peck's Road for 1.8 miles to line, then for another 1.7 miles to Bull Hill Road.

6.7   Left on Bull Hill Road for 0.9 miles to Route 7.

7.6   Left on Route 7 for 2.6 miles.

10.2   Go right at sign to Greylock Reservation (North Main Street) bearing right on Quarry Road for 1.2 miles to Rockwell Road.

11.4   Left on Rockwell Road for 0.7 miles to visitor's center.

12.1   Total mileage.

Ride 20B: Williamstown to Visitor's Center

0.0   From Field Park head south on Route 7 for 13.9 miles and the sign to Greylock Reservation on left to North Main Street.

13.9   Go left on North Main Street bearing right on Quarry Road for 1.2 miles to Rockwell Road.

15.1   Go left on Rockwell Road for 0.7 miles to visitor's center.

15.8   Total mileage.

Ride 20C: North Adams to Visitor's Center, westerly route

0.0   From the Sheraton Inn go 0.2 miles up West Main to its intersection with Route 2.

0.2   Go left on Route 2 for 0.1 miles to Notch Road entrance to the reservation and keep going for another 0.3 miles to Roberts Drive.

1.5   Go right on Roberts Drive for 0.2 miles to the intersection with Massachusetts Avenue.

1.7   Go left on Massachusetts Ave for 3.1 miles to Cole Ave.

4.8   Turn left on Cole Avenue for 0.7 miles.

5.5   Turn right on Route 2 for 0.1 miles to Water Street.

5.6   Go left on Water Street for 4.8 miles along Green River Road to Steele's Corners.

10.4   Turn left on Route 7 at Steele's Corners for 9.6 miles to sign to visitor's center and North Main Street.

20.0   Turn left on North Main Street, bearing right on Quarry Road for 1.2 miles to Rockwell Road.

21.2   Go left on Rockwell Road for 0.7 miles to visitor's center.

21.9   Total mileage.

Ride 20D: North Adams to Visitor's Center, easterly route

0.0   From the Sheraton Inn head south on American Legion Drive.

0.3   Go right on Ashland Street for 1.2 miles bearing right at Getty station and another 1.2 miles to East Road intersection.

2.7   Bear left on East Road and continue 5.7 miles to intersection with Route 116.

8.4   Go right on Route 116 for 0.3 miles.

8.7   Go left on Wells Road for 3.5 miles.

12.2   Turn right on Main Street, Cheshire, for 0.5 miles until intersection with Route 8.

12.7   Go left on Route 8 for 0.3 miles.

13.0   Go right on Lanesboro Road for 4.3 miles.

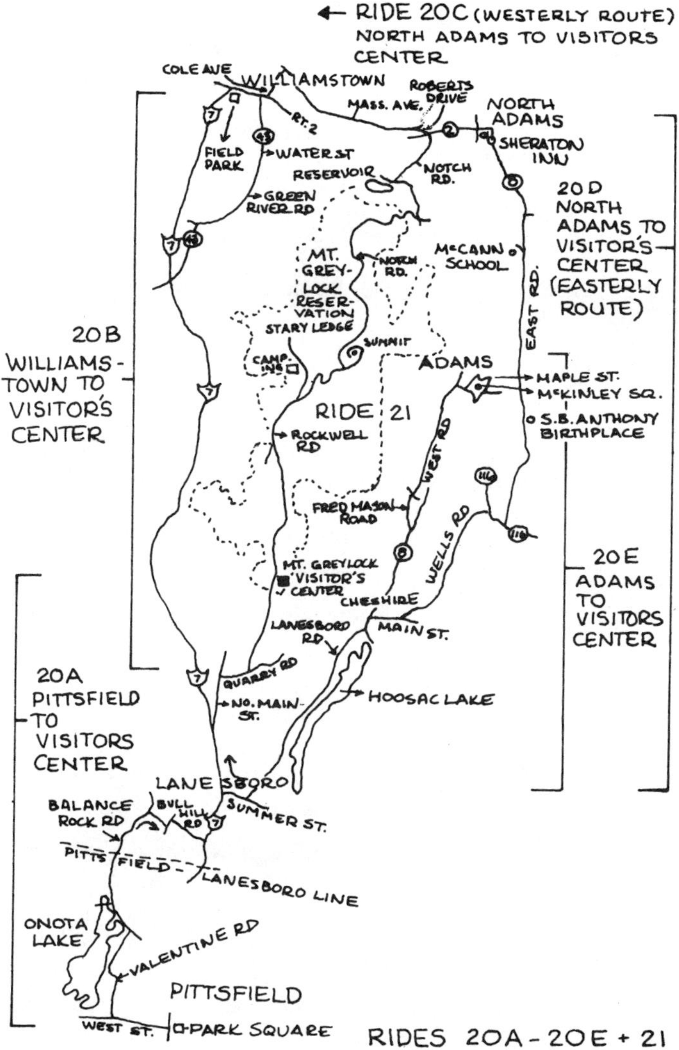

RIDES 20A - 20E + 21
UP AND OVER
MT. GREYLOCK

17.3   Go right at stop sign at T for a 0.3 mile climb to top of hill and then a long downhill to Route 7 for a total 0.6 miles.

17.9   Go right on Route 7, heading north for 1.4 miles to sign for visitor's center.

19.3   Go right on North Main Street, bearing right on Quarry Road for 1.2 miles to Rockwell Road.

20.5   Turn left on Rockwell Road for 0.7 miles to visitor's center.

21.2   Total mileage.

Ride 20E: Adams to Visitor's Center

0.0   Start at McKinley Square and head west up Maple Street for 0.4 miles and intersection with West Road.

0.4   Go left on West Road for 3.5 miles to intersection of Fred Mason Road and Route 8.

3.9   Go right, south on Route 8 for 1.0 miles to Lanesboro Road.

4.9   Turn right on Lanesboro Road for 4.3 miles.

9.2   Go right at stop sign at T for a 0.3 mile climb to top of hill and then the long downhill to Route 7, total 0.6 miles.

9.8   Go right on Route 7, heading north for 1.4 miles to sign for visitor's center, Mount Greylock Reservation.

11.2   Go right on North Main Street, bearing right on Quarry Road for 1.2 miles to Rockwell Road.

12.4   Go left on Rockwell Road for 0.7 miles to visitor's center.

13.1   Total mileage.

Ride 21: Up and Over the "High Lord of the Berkshires"

17.7 miles

The ride to the Mount Greylock summit, 8.3 miles from the visitor's center, is a long pull with the steeper part at the very beginning. The pavement, however, is smooth, so the trip means settling down in a low gear and taking your time to get to the top.

At the 5.8 mile mark there's a dirt road turnoff to the Stony Ledge campground which is 0.6 miles in; or if you want to go to the end of the ledge where there's a bare rock lookout and Adirondack shelter, the distance is 1.6 miles.

Dirt roads are not recommended for bicycling, especially with loads. But the trip out to the end of Stony Ledge, which is uphill a bit, is definitely worth making as it provides an unusual view of the summit. The road ends in a cul-de-sac. Look sharply for a trail leading to the Adirondack shelter, about 30 yards from the parking area. The blueberrying is good if you're there at the right time.

If you don't make the turnoff to Stony Ledge, but keep going straight, Notch Road intersects Rockwell Road at the 7.4 mile mark. Keep going up until you reach the summit. Along this last leg is a superb view of Adams, lying almost immediately below.

On the trip down, take the right on Notch Road for 6.9 downhill miles, the steepest part being near the bottom. Your brakes will be needed. At the Bernard Farm, almost immediately after leaving the gates of the reservation, turn left for another 1.2 downhill miles to the Mount Williams Reservoir. Just before the reservoir, go right on Notch Road for 1.3 miles back to Route 2 coming out of North Adams.

Go left for Williamstown, 0.3 miles to Roberts Drive where the ride turns right, then left on Massachusetts Avenue and left on Cole Avenue as in the North Adams to visitor's center westerly route.

Go right for North Adams, following Route 2 for 1.2 miles into the business center. For Adams, pick up the North Adams to visitor's center easterly route, but stay on East Road for only 2.1 miles. Turn right on Lime Street, head downhill 0.2 miles, then left on North Summer Street

Mt. Greylock War Memorial stands at summit of highest peak in Massachusetts. Visitors can ascend tower on inside.

for 1.1 miles, right on Hoosac Street for 0.2 miles and left on Park Street for 0.1 miles to McKinley Square.

If you are headed back to Pittsfield you can take either the North Adams easterly or westerly route. The westerly is 26.2 miles and the flatter of the two. The easterly is 25.1, but hillier.

Summary: Ride 21

0.0   Visitor's center.

5.8   Turnoff to Stony Ledge (keep going straight for summit). At 1.6 miles intersection with Notch Road from North Adams.

7.4   At Notch Road intersection go straight to summit, 0.9 miles.

8.3   Summit.

9.2   Back to intersection with Notch Road, go right 5.9 miles.

15.1   You reach the gates to the reservation.

15.2   At Bernard Farm go left 1.2 miles to reservoir.

16.4   Go right on Notch Road 1.3 miles to Route 2.

17.7   Total mileage.

Turnoff to Stony Ledge

0.6   To campground, round trip is 1.2 miles.

1.6   To Stony Ledge lookout and the Adirondack shelter, round trip is 3.2 miles.

Photograph by Christopher Ormond

Chapter 6:
Northern Berkshire:
Mount Greylock Surrounded

There's hardly a bicycle ride that can be taken in northern Berkshire County without at least one view of Mount Greylock. That's because the state's highest peak, described in the previous chapter, juts up between two other mountain ranges — the Hoosac and the Taconic — that define northern Berkshire. The result is terrain that is narrow valley and mountain, with the most level areas in the vicinity of Williamstown.

On some rides Mount Greylock presents a long, sweeping profile, such as in the view from East Road high above Adams, or from Route 7 just south of Williamstown. Sometimes the view is almost foreshortened, as it is when heading north from Cheshire, and sometimes you ride almost underneath the mountain, as on West Road in Adams. But because of Mount Greylock, the riding terrain in north Berkshire is horseshoe shaped, with the curve at the top formed by Williamstown and North Adams and the sides created by Adams and Cheshire and South Williamstown, New Ashford and Hancock.

Northern Berkshire has other attractions for the rider. Adams has a lovely Quaker Meeting House, situated in the dignified setting of Maple Street Cemetery in the shadow of Mount Greylock, and it also boasts the birthplace of Susan B. Anthony on West Road, as well as magnificent views. North Adams has a lovely camping area on Windsor Lake, the city's recreational area, only about a mile from the downtown, and a burgeoning craft and artisan center in the Old Windsor Mill. As this book went to press the city had embarked on plans for a Hoosac Tunnel Museum, the restoration of parts of its downtown and the rebuilding of parts of its business area.

Williamstown is a classic New England town, dominated by the First Congregational Church on its main street, wide lawns and the stately buildings of Williams College. What many critics regard as the best summer theater in the United States takes place in July and August, and a visit to the Sterling and Francine Clark Art Institute, known throughout the world for its collection of nineteenth century French art, is a must. Aside from all of that, the dozen or so restaurants in the Williamstown area are ranked among the top in New England.

Both North Adams and Adams have an industrial heritage because the Hoosac River powered the textile mills that shaped their histories. Both have ample shopping areas for the basics, while Williamstown's offerings include more specialty oriented merchandise.

Thumbnail sketches of the area's better known tourist attractions follow.

Hoosac Tunnel, North Adams

The Hoosac Tunnel, which goes 4½ miles underneath the Hoosac Mountain range just east of North Adams, is not included on any rides because its western portal in North Adams is virtually inaccessible to everyone but hikers. Construction of the tunnel from 1851 to 1875 was considered one of the major engineering feats of the nineteenth century, and when completed the tunnel linked Albany, New York, to Boston, transforming North Adams into a major railroad center. Until 1916, it was the longest tunnel in North America. As this guide went to press efforts were being made in North Adams to establish a museum to tell the story of the tunnel's construction.

Hoosuck Community Resources Corp., Windsor Mill, North Adams.

Hoosuck is a somewhat loosely organized association of citizens and working crafts people located in a former textile mill on Union Street, North Adams. At this writing more than a dozen enterprises, ranging from silversmithing to stained glass, occupy the mill. Information about the mill and the individual studios may be obtained at the main office on Union Street. At one time guided tours were conducted on a regular basis, and they may be reinstated at a future date, so a check is worthwhile if you are interested in learning about a somewhat unique effort to make an old mill work again.

Jiminy Peak (Alpine Slide), Hancock. (See Rides 22 and 27).

Located just off Route 43, the Jiminy Peak Ski Area in Hancock offers an Alpine Slide during the warm weather months. The slide is a one or two person sled with controls that descends a five-eighths mile track down the mountain. Riders get to the start via chairlift. The facility is operated daily during July and August, weekends only in the spring and fall. Tickets are $2.50 with option plans for lower prices.

Natural Bridge, North Adams

Located about two miles north of the center of North Adams just off Route 8, the Natural Bridge is the only natural marble bridge in North America and is estimated to be about 550 million years old. It was formed by Hudson Brook literally boring a hole through the rock in a process that took thousands of years. The facility is open daily during the summer months and admission is $1.

Quaker Meeting House, Adams. (See Rides 23 and 23A).

Built in 1782 by the Quakers who first settled in Adams, the unpainted, wooden frame Quaker Meeting House stands in the dignified setting of the Maple Street Cemetery, with Mount Greylock as its backdrop. The interior of the building is not open except for an annual worship service each fall by the Society of Friends.

Sterling and Francine Clark Art Institute, Williamstown. (See Rides 25 and 26).

The Clark houses one of the world's foremost collections of nineteenth century French art and is one of the major tourist attractions in the county. The collection includes paintings by Renoir, Monet, Degas, Corot, Sargent, Homer and Remington, as well as a fine collection of English and American silver. The facility, which includes galleries, a theater and a library, is open Tuesday through Sunday from 10 a.m. to 5 p.m. and is closed Mondays except for Memorial Day, Labor Day and Columbus Day. Admission is free.

Susan B. Anthony's Birthplace, Adams. (See Rides 22, 23 and 23A).

Susan B. Anthony, the leader of the women's suffrage movement in the United States, was born in 1820 in Adams, at the home that stands on the corner of East and Walling Roads. Because of private ownership it is not open to the public, but a plaque marks its historic nature.

Williams College Museum of Art, Williamstown. (See Rides 24, 25, 26 and 27).

Route 2 threads through the Williams College campus whose stately trees and ample lawns make Williamstown a town with classic New England looks. The college art museum is located on Route 2, just east of Spring Street. The permanent collection is regarded as excellent, and its exhibits change often. The museum is open daily from 10 a.m. to noon and 2 to 4 p.m., Sundays from 2 to 5 p.m., but is closed July 4, Labor Day and on college holidays. Admission is free. Another attraction worth investigating on the Williams campus is the Milham planetarium.

Williamstown Theatre Festival, Williamstown. (See Rides 24, 25, 26 and 27).

The Williamstown Theatre Festival, in its 25th anniversary year in 1979, offers a whole host of activities during July and August ranging from main stage performances to the singing of the Cabaret group in area restaurants. The quality of its productions throughout the years has earned the festival a national reputation for excellence. As a result, it is ranked among the major tourist attractions in the county. The theater is located on Route 2, near the center of town.

Windsor Lake, North Adams

The recreation area for the city of North Adams, Windsor Lake is located up a steep hill about a mile from Main Street. Facilities include swimming and camping.

Ride 22: Greylock Go-Around

39.4 miles

This 40-mile ride incorporates all of the other rides in northern Berkshire, going completely around Mount Greylock by heading south from North Adams to Adams and Cheshire, and then west over Mount Greylock's southern flank to Lanesboro, then north to Williamstown and east to North Adams.

The ride starts at the Sheraton Inn in North Adams and heads south on American Legion Drive for 0.3 miles to Ashland Street, where it goes right for 1.2 miles past the

North Adams State College apartment dormitories to a Getty station where the ride bears right for another 1.2 miles to the East Road intersection with McCann Regional Vocational School just ahead and on the left.

Go left on East Road, leaving McCann School on the right, and prepare to climb gradually, with some flat and some steep places, for 5.7 miles to the intersection with Route 116. At 6.3 miles from the ride's start, at East Road's intersection with Walling Road, stands the house where Susan B. Anthony was born. It is privately owned and therefore not open to the public, but a plaque marks its historic nature. The toughest climb, near the end of this stretch at 7.1 miles from the start, involves nearly a half-mile that might have to be walked. The reward is a rest stop near a farm house at top where riders can take in a sweeping view to the east and south while enjoying a deserved rest and anticipating a four-mile downhill run to Cheshire.

Coast down from the farmhouse to Route 116, take a right for 0.3 miles, then a left on Wells Road in Cheshire, a nice, long and easy downhill to the town's Main Street, where you go right for 0.5 miles until its intersection with Route 8. Go left on Route 8 for 0.3 miles, then right on Lanesboro Road for 4.3 miles, a gradual rolling climb on the high side of Hoosac Lake.

The road ends at a "T" where the ride goes right 0.3 miles to the top of the hill and then a half-mile coast down to the intersection of Route 7, where a right turn heads north to Williamstown and a left to Pittsfield. Take the right, following Route 7, a wide, well-paved road. At 1.4 miles on this leg North Main Street heads off to the right leading to the entrance of the Mount Greylock Reservation. At 2.8 miles the ride can go left over the Brodie Mountain Road (follow signs to Jiminy Peak), a steep, but scenic climb over the mountain to Hancock that will extend the overall ride about three miles. If you choose not to extend the ride, continue straight on Route 7 to Steele's Corners, the intersection of Routes 7 and 43, take a right over the Green River Road into Williamstown, or keep going straight up the Route 7 hill to Williamstown. The latter will afford a spectacular view of Mount Greylock's "hopper" section if you don't mind another climb.

To backtrack a bit, there are variations. The ride over

Brodie Mountain Road to Jiminy Peak is 3.4 miles, then go right on Route 43, a rolling but gradual downhill to Steele's Corners and then Williamstown. At Steele's Corners the climb up Route 7 will give a magnificent view of Mount Greylock. The ride from Steele's Corners along Green River Road avoids the uphill and is very pretty because the road follows the river to Williamstown, going gradually downhill for 4.8 miles to Route 2.

Whether you come in to Route 2 from Route 7 or from the Green River Road (Route 43), which becomes Water Street in Williamstown, head towards North Adams to Cole Avenue, 0.1 miles from the Route 43 intersection, then go left for 0.7 miles and right on North Hoosac Road for 3.1 miles, going straight where Roberts Drive veers off to the right and over a hill that then dips down into River Street in North Adams. At Marshall Street in North Adams go right for 0.2 miles back to the Sheraton Inn.

The total distance for the ride is 39.4 miles, but if the Brodie Mountain Road-Route 43 extension is taken, it totals 43.1 miles.

Summary: Ride 22

0.0   From the Sheraton Inn in North Adams, head south on American Legion Drive.

0.3   Go right on Ashland Street for 1.2 miles, bearing right at the Getty station, and another 1.2 miles to East Road intersection.

2.7   Go left on East Road and continue 5.7 miles to the intersection with Route 116.

8.4   Go right at Route 116 for 0.3 miles.

8.7   Left at Wells Road for 3.5 miles.

12.2   Right on Main Street, Cheshire, for 0.5 miles until intersection with Route 8.

12.7   Go left on Route 8 for 0.3 miles.

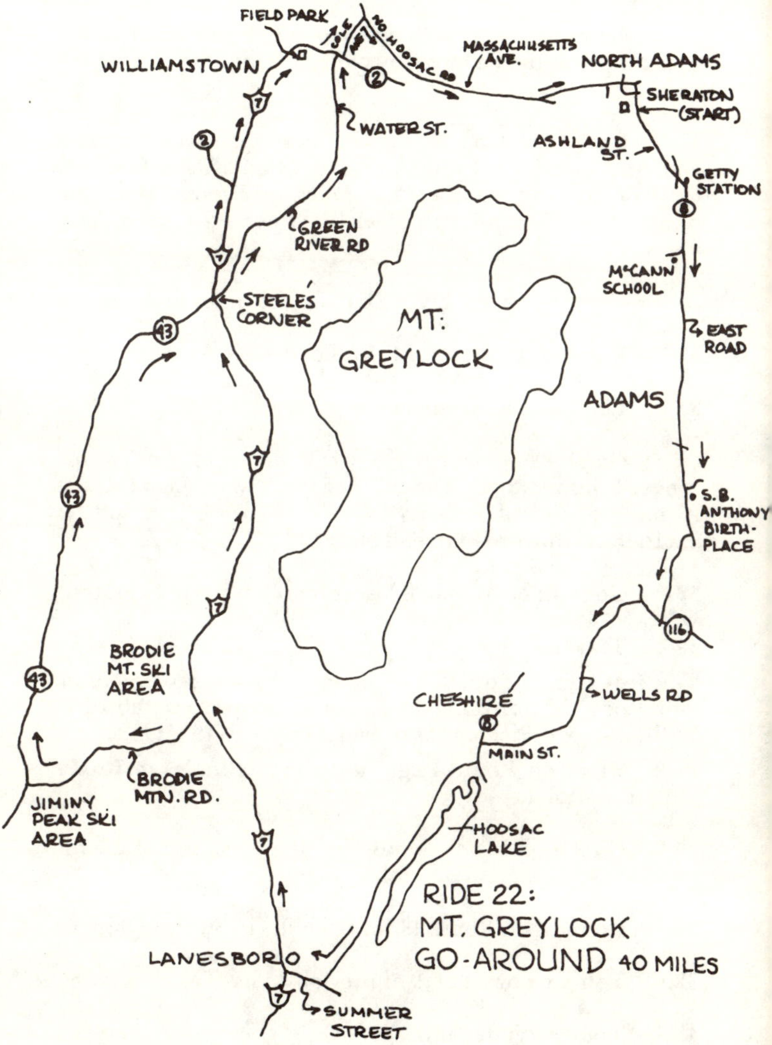
FIELD PARK
WILLIAMSTOWN
NO. HOOSAC RD
MASSACHUSETTS AVE.
NORTH ADAMS
SHERATON (START)
WATER ST.
ASHLAND ST.
GETTY STATION
GREEN RIVER RD
McCANN SCHOOL
STEELE'S CORNER
MT. GREYLOCK
EAST ROAD
ADAMS
S.B. ANTHONY BIRTH-PLACE
BRODIE MT. SKI AREA
CHESHIRE
WELLS RD
MAIN ST.
BRODIE MTN. RD.
JIMINY PEAK SKI AREA
HOOSAC LAKE
LANESBORO
SUMMER STREET
RIDE 22: MT. GREYLOCK GO-AROUND 40 MILES

13.0   Go right on Lanesboro Road for 4.3 miles.

17.3   Go right at stop sign at T, for a 0.3 mile climb to top of the hill and then a long downhill to Route 7, a total of 0.6 miles.

17.9   Go right on Route 7, heading back towards Williamstown for 1.4 miles to North Main St. and Greylock Reservation and another 2.8 miles to Brodie Mountain Road. Then 6.8 miles to Steele's Corners, a total of 11.0 miles.

28.9   Right on Green River Road for 4.8 miles to Route 2.

33.7   Right on Route 2 for 0.1 miles to Cole Avenue.

33.8   Left on Cole Avenue for 0.7 miles.

34.5   Go right on North Hoosac Road for 3.1 miles and proceed into North Adams, bear left on Massachusetts Avenue instead of Roberts Drive and go over the hill for another 1.6 miles to Marshall Street.

39.2   Go right on Marshall Street for 0.2 miles to Sheraton.

39.4   Total mileage.

This ride can be extended by taking a left on Brodie Mountain Road and crossing to Route 43 to proceed north to Williamstown. Pick up the previous trip at 17.9 miles.

17.9   Right on Route 7, go north for 2.8 miles to Brodie Mountain Road.

20.7   Go left on Brodie Mountain Road over top of the hill to Route 43, a total of 3.4 miles.

24.1   Go right on Route 43 for 8.5 miles to Steele's Corners.

32.6   You are now at 28.9 of previous ride.

43.1   Total extended mileage.

Rides 23, 23A, 24, 25, 26 and 27 are based on the Greylock Go-Around described in the previous section, but offer cutoffs or variations.

Ride 23: North Adams to Cheshire to Adams Ramble

25 miles

The ride follows the first section of Ride 22, heading south from the Sheraton Inn over East Road in Adams, then a short hop on Route 116 to Wells Road and then the long downhill into Cheshire's Main Street and its intersection with Route 8.

But at Route 8, instead of turning left as in Ride 22, go right, following the main road for 1.8 miles and watching for Fred Mason Road, which bears off obliquely to the left. There's a steady but gradual climb as Fred Mason Road heads north to the Adams-Cheshire line where it becomes West Road, a 3.5 mile route that takes you around the very base of Mount Greylock and allows a view over the top of Adams to the East Road, the route taken in the beginning of the ride.

Go right on Maple Street where almost immediately you'll see the Quaker Meeting House in the middle of the cemetery and head downhill for 0.4 miles to McKinley Square, dominated by the statue of President McKinley in tribute to his visit to Adams during his term in office. Go left for 0.1 miles, then right on Hoosac Street for 0.3 miles, then left on North Summer Street for 1.1 miles and right on Lime Street up a hill for 0.2 miles, then left. This brings the ride back to East Road, the starting part, and from the top of the short rise just after leaving Lime Street it is an easy 2.1 miles downhill to South Church Street in North Adams where the ride bears left onto Ashland Street for 1.2 miles to American Legion Drive, then left for 0.3 miles back to the Sheraton Inn, for a total of 25 miles.

Ride 23A

12.1 miles

Ride 23A is a shortened version that starts at McKinley Square in Adams, heads south on Park Street for 0.3 miles

Quaker Meeting House in Adams is at top of Maple Street with Mt. Greylock in background.

and then straight on Orchard Street, which becomes Route 116, for a two mile climb to Wells Road, then right to Cheshire and Route 8, right on Route 8 and left on Fred Mason Road back to West Road and Adams as described in Ride 23. The ride is 12.1 miles.

A second variation is to start at McKinley Square, go right on Hoosac, left on North Summer, and right on Lime as described in Ride 23. But then go right on East Road, instead of left, taking it to the intersection of Route 116, a leg of about 3.5 miles, then right on Route 116 for a downhill coast into Adams for 2.3 miles. Another 0.3 miles along Park Street takes the ride back to McKinley Square for a total mileage of 7.8.

Summary: Ride 23

0.0   From the Sheraton Inn, North Adams, head south on American Legion Drive.

0.3   Go right on Ashland Street for 1.2 miles, bearing right at the Getty station for another 1.2 miles to East Road intersection.

2.7   Go left on East Road and continue 5.7 miles to intersection with Route 116.

8.4   Go right on Route 116 for 0.3 miles.

8.7   Left on Wells Road for 3.5 miles.

12.2   Right on Main Street, Cheshire, for 0.5 miles until intersection with Route 8.

12.7   Right on Route 8 for 1.9 miles to Fred Mason Road on left.

14.6   Follow Fred Mason Road to town line and West Road, 3.5 miles.

18.1   Right on Maple Street and downhill for 0.4 miles.

18.5   Left at McKinley Square for 0.1 miles.

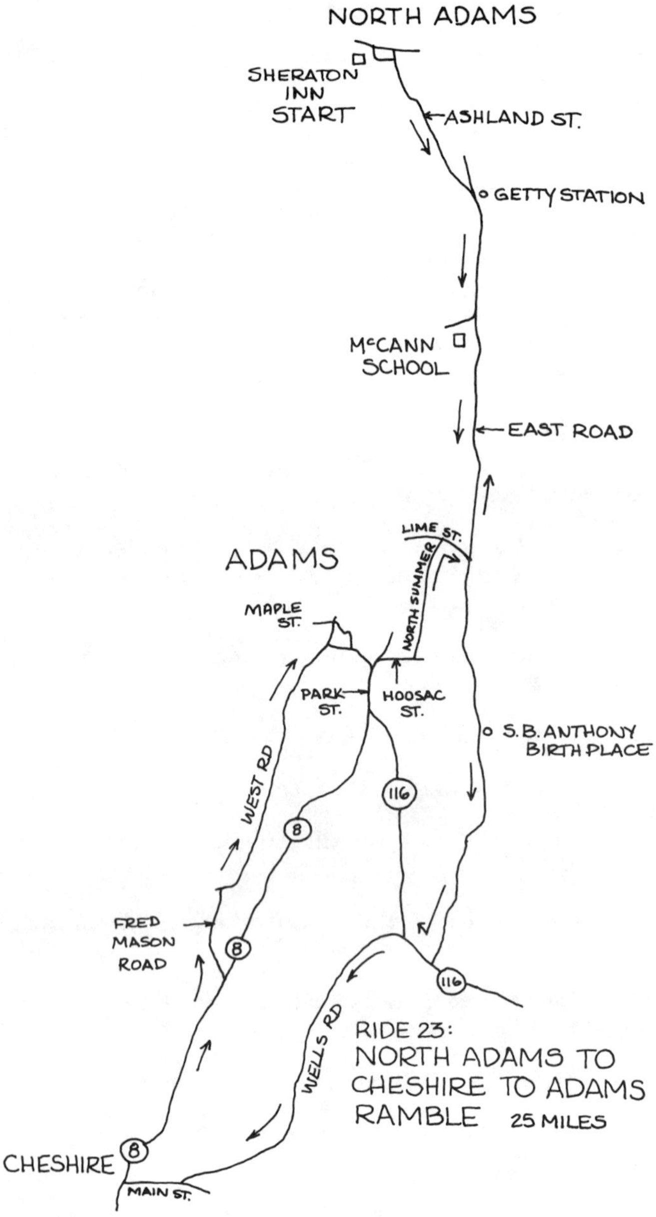
NORTH ADAMS
SHERATON INN START
ASHLAND ST.
GETTY STATION
McCANN SCHOOL
EAST ROAD
LIME ST.
NORTH SUMMER
ADAMS
MAPLE ST.
PARK ST.
HOOSAC ST.
S. B. ANTHONY BIRTH PLACE
WEST RD
116
8
FRED MASON ROAD
WELLS RD
CHESHIRE
MAIN ST.
RIDE 23:
NORTH ADAMS TO CHESHIRE TO ADAMS RAMBLE
25 MILES

18.6   Right at Hoosac Street for 0.3 miles.

18.9   Left on North Summer Street for 1.1 miles.

20.0   Right on Lime Street uphill for 0.2 miles.

20.2   Left on East Road for 2.1 miles to South Church Street.

22.3   Right on South Church Street for 1.2 miles then bear left 1.2 miles to American Legion Drive.

24.7   Left at American Legion Drive 0.3 miles back to the Sheraton.

25.0   Total mileage.

Summary: Ride 23A

0.0   Start at McKinley Square, head south on Park Street for 0.3 miles.

0.3   Straight on Orchard Street to Route 116 and start a long climb for 2.0 miles to Wells Road and go right. Pick up Ride 23 at 8.7 mile mark and end at 18.5.

12.1   Total mileage.

Ride 24: North Adams to Williamstown and Back
21.1 miles

The ride begins at the Sheraton Inn and heads north for 0.2 miles on Marshall Street, leaving the Mohawk Center on the left. At the traffic light go left on River Street and almost immediately start climbing a short hill. Then go over generally flat terrain through the North Adams' west end for a total of 4.7 miles to the intersection with Cole Avenue in Williamstown.

Go left on Cole Avenue for 0.7 miles, then right on Route 2, and up a short hill going through the Williams College campus to the intersection of Routes 2 and 7 at Field Park, the location of the Williams Inn. Head south on Routes 7 and 2, staying on 7 past the Mt. Greylock Regional High School, a route that affords a sweeping view of Mount Greylock and its "Hopper" section, a scoop formed by Mount Greylock and smaller mountains. This 4.3 mile leg ends at Steele's Corners, the intersection of Routes 7 and 43, at the bottom of a downhill. Go left on Route 43, which is also called Green River Road, a scenic country road that follows the river for 4.8 miles back to Route 2 in Williamstown where the beginning of the ride is retraced. This means a right on Route 2 for 0.1 miles, a left on Cole Avenue for 0.7 miles, then a right on North Hoosac Road for the 4.9 mile ride back to North Adams. If you choose to bear right on Roberts Drive in North Adams, which will take you to Route 2 going into the center of town, the final hill can be avoided. But heavy traffic going into North Adams will almost certainly be encountered as a penalty.

Summary: Ride 24

0.0   From the Sheraton Inn, head north on Marshall Street for 0.2 miles.

0.2   Left on River Street for 4.7 miles.

4.9   Left on Cole Avenue for 0.7 miles.

5.6   Right on Route 2 for 0.7 miles to Field Park and Route 7.

North Adams is second city in the Berkshires with population of about 18,000. View is Main Street looking east towards Monument Square.

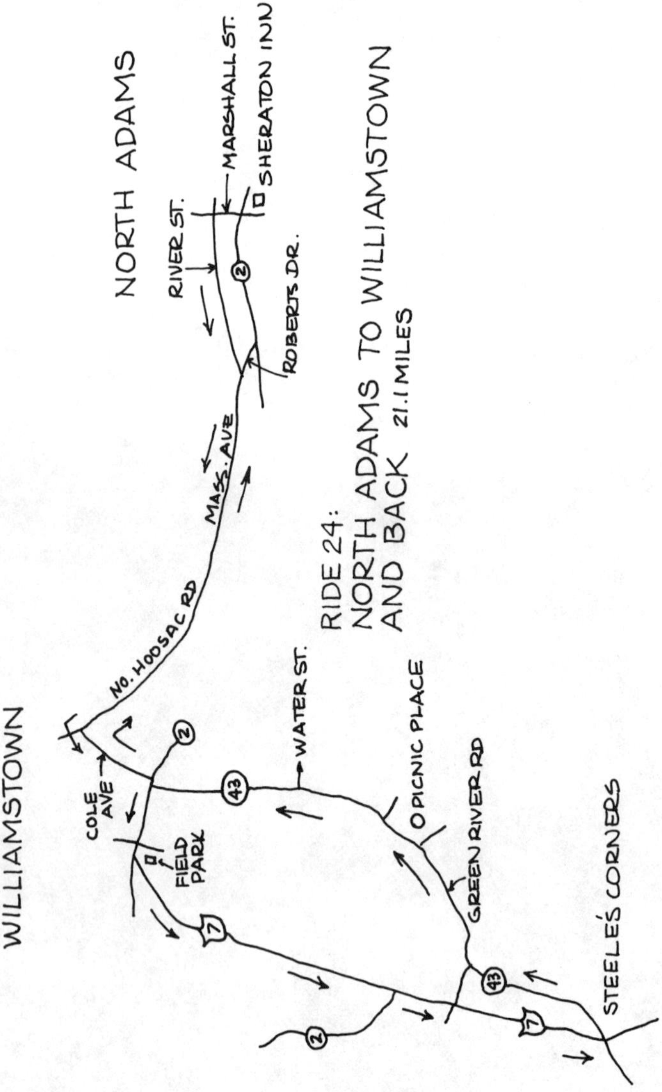
NORTH ADAMS
WILLIAMSTOWN
RIDE 24:
NORTH ADAMS TO WILLIAMSTOWN
AND BACK
21.1 MILES
MARSHALL ST.
SHERATON INN
RIVER ST.
ROBERTS DR.
MASS. AVE
NO. HOOSAC RD
COLE AVE
FIELD PARK
WATER ST.
PICNIC PLACE
GREEN RIVER RD
STEELE'S CORNERS
2
43
7

6.3 Head west on Route 7 for 4.3 miles and Steele's Corners.

10.6 Go left on Green River Road for 4.8 miles to Route 2.

15.4 Go right on Route 2 for 0.1 miles.

15.5 Left on Cole Avenue for 0.7 miles.

16.2 Right on North Hoosac Road for 4.7 miles.

20.9 Right on Marshall Street for 0.2 miles back to the Sheraton Inn.

21.1 Total Mileage.

Ride 25: Williamstown Short Loop
3.4 miles

This is an easy ride within Williamstown, taking the visitor to the Clark Art Institute and through pretty residential surroundings. It starts at Field Park where the Williams Inn is located and heads south on South Street for 0.4 miles to the art institute.

The ride then continues for 1.3 miles along Gale Road, with the Taconic Golf course on its left, to the intersection with Green River Road where it goes left for 1.1 miles back to Route 2, or Main Street, and then another left for 0.6 miles back to Field Park. A variation is to take Latham Street, which goes left from Route 43, now Water Street, into Spring Street, Williamstown's main shopping street, and then to Route 2 and left back to Field Park.

Summary: Ride 25

0.0   From Field Park head west on South Street.

0.4   Clark Art Museum.

1.7   Intersection with Green River Rd. Go left for 1.1 mi.

2.8   Go left on Route 2 for 0.6 miles back to Field Park.

3.4   Total mileage.

**RIDE 25:
WILLIAMSTOWN
SHORT LOOP
3.4 MILES**

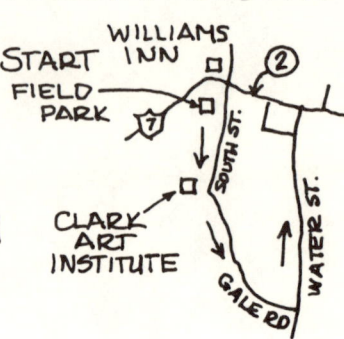

Clark Art Institute on South Street, Williamstown, is home of one of world's foremost collections of 19th Century French art. Photo is of older section.

Ride 26: Williamstown Longer Loop

11.1 miles

This ride makes a nice leisurely morning or afternoon tour, giving the flavor of New England back roads. Part of the route, however, is on dirt road so that the ride should be avoided if conditions are excessively wet.

The ride begins at the Williams Inn and heads south on Routes 7 and 2, going straight where Route 2 heads right into New York State at the 2.4 mile mark. At 3.0 miles go right on Woodcock Road, flat for a while then up a short hill, and straight at the top along Oblong Road where the surface turns to dirt. Go 2.5 miles to the intersection with Sloan Road where the ride goes left and down a delightful 1.2 mile hill to Steele's Corners, the intersection of Routes 7 and 43.

Follow the Green River Road (Route 43) for 4.8 miles back to Route 2, and then left on Route 2 for 0.6 miles back to Field Park. Total mileage is 11.1 miles.

The ride can be varied to include a visit to the Clark Art Institute by following Green River Road for 3.7 miles from Steele's Corners to the intersection with Gale Road. Take a left, climb a hill and go for 1.3 miles to the Clark. From there follow South Street to Field Park for 0.4 miles.

Summary: Ride 26

0.0   From Field Park head west and south on Routes 7 and 2.

2.4   Route 2 heads into New York. Go straight.

3.0   Go right on Woodcock Road. Proceed 2.5 miles and bear left on Oblong Road.

4.5   Left on Sloan Road down long hill 1.2 miles to Steele's Corners.

5.7   Follow Green River 4.8 miles to Route 2, (passing Mount Hope Park).

10.5   Go left on Route 2 for 0.6 miles back to Field Park.

Regulation House in Field Park, Williamstown, is replica of settlement's first houses. Structure was built with authentic materials and tools for town's bicentennial celebration.

11.1   Total mileage.
OR
5.7   Follow Green River 3.7 miles to intersection with Gale Road.

9.4   Go left on Gale 1.3 miles to Clark Art Institute.

10.7   Take South Street to Field Park 0.4 miles.

11.1   Total mileage.

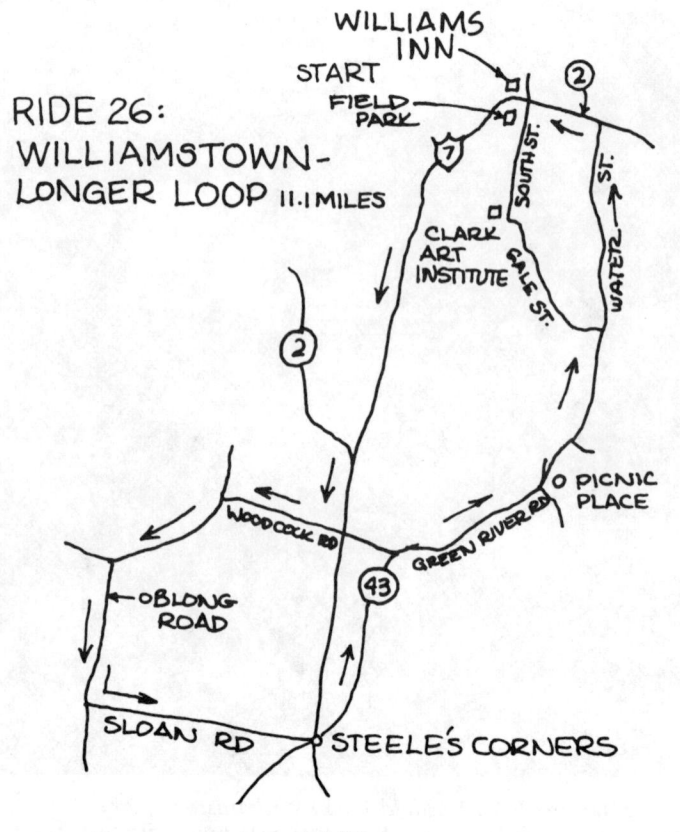

RIDE 26:
WILLIAMSTOWN-
LONGER LOOP 11.1 MILES

Ride 27: Figure 8 High-Low from Williamstown to Hancock to New Ashford and Back.

25.4 miles

From Field Park follow Routes 7 and 2 south, but keep on Route 7 for 11.1 miles, going past the Brodie Mountain Ski Area on the right. At the intersection of the Brodie Mountain Road with Route 7 there will be Jiminy Peak signs pointing to the right.

Go right on the Brodie Mountain Road up a steep one-mile climb and then downhill 2.9 miles to Jiminy Peak, where an Alpine Slide offers rides in the warmer months. Just beyond Jiminy you will come to the intersection of Route 43.

Go right on Route 43 for 8.5 miles back to Steele's Corners, a gradual but rolling downhill, then cross the intersection of Route 7 and follow the Green River Road for 4.8 miles back to Route 2. Go left on Route 2 for 0.6 miles back to Field Park, for a total mileage of 25.4.

Summary: Ride 27

0.0 From Field Park follow Route 7 west and south 11.1 miles. Follow signs to Alpine Slide and Jiminy Peak.

11.1 Go right on Brodie Mountain Road, for a steep one-mile climb, then downhill 2.9 miles to Jiminy and 3.4 miles to stop sign at Route 43.

14.5 Turn right on Route 43 for 8.5 miles to Steele's Corners.

23.0 Go straight on Green River Road for 4.8 miles to Route 2.

24.8 Go left on Route 2 to Field Park for 0.6 miles.

25.4 Total mileage.

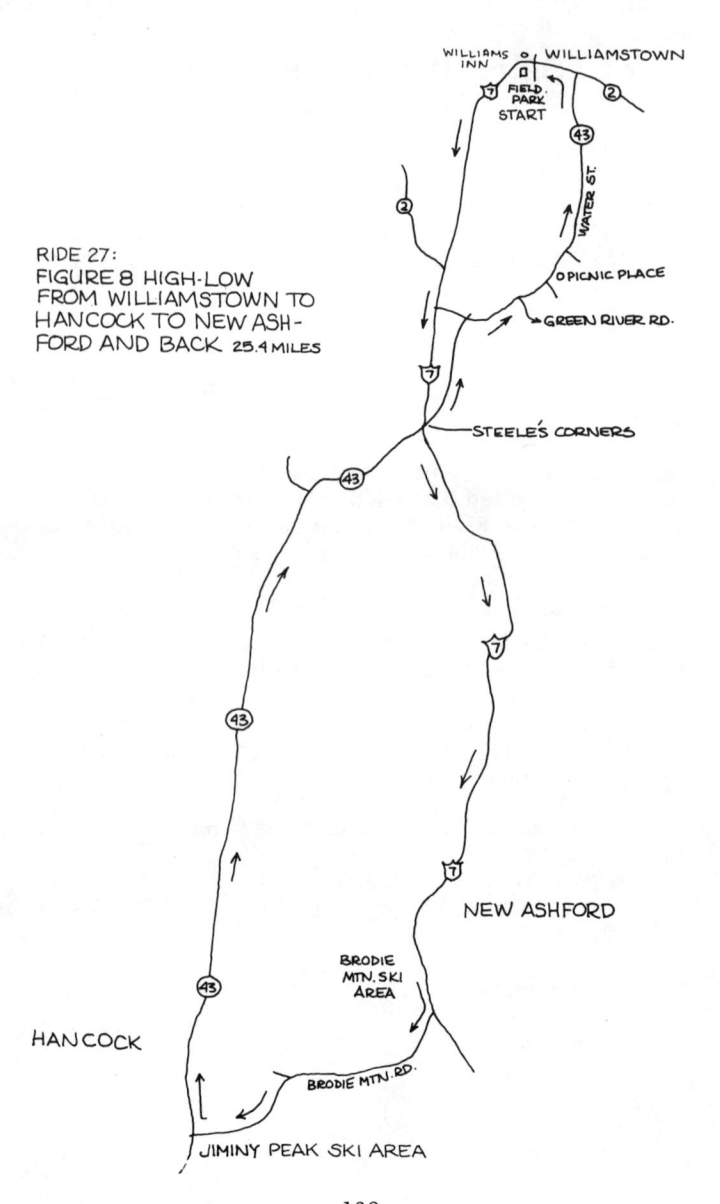

RIDE 27:
FIGURE 8 HIGH-LOW FROM WILLIAMSTOWN TO HANCOCK TO NEW ASHFORD AND BACK 25.4 MILES

"The Hopper" section of Mt. Greylock is a spectacular view, no matter what season. This photo was taken in early spring from Route 7, just south of Williamstown.

In background is Mt. Everett, highest mountain in southern Berkshire.

Chapter 7:
Putting It All Together:
Two Weeks On Berkshire Byways

Berkshire County lends itself to an unhurried two-week bicycle trip that offers an unusual variety of experiences. What follows is a two-week itinerary with suggested stops to incorporate the best camping, dining, lodging and entertainment, with days off for rest.

With some hesitancy, a number of places are mentioned for overnight lodging. The hesitancy comes because the author, a resident of Berkshire County, has never stayed overnight at one of its hotels, motels or guest houses, and therefore cannot in good conscience make recommendations. The places mentioned are either centrally located or just plain well known.

Details on both camping places and lodgings may be obtained from the Berkshire Hills Conference as explained in Chapter 1.

Assuming you are armed with the specifics, here are suggestions for a two-week ride with ample vacation rewards, even though the hills won't always be down.

Saturday

Arrive in Sheffield, staying either at Stagecoach Hill on Route 41 between Salisbury, Connecticut, and Great Barrington, Massachusetts, or at the Orchard Shade Guest House just off Route 7 in Sheffield Center. After checking in take Ride 1, the Sheffield Swing Around, as a warm-up, making whatever bicycle adjustments are needed for the longer trips ahead.

Sunday

Pack up your camping gear and plan to spend Sunday night in the Beartown State Forest, just east of Great Barrington. Start on Ride 1, following County Road east from Route 7, going through the covered bridge and climbing the long gradual hill to the intersection of the Mill River-Great Barrington Road, distinguished by the woods-and-brush filled triangle. The distance from Route 7 to the intersection is 5.7 miles.

Then instead of going right to Mill River as in Ride 1, go straight ahead and down a short hill, then right to the intersection of Route 57, a distance of 2.5 miles from the triangle intersection. At Route 57 go left and ride past Lake Buel on your left for 3.2 miles to the intersection with Route 23. Go right on Route 23 for a mile to the entrance of the Beartown State Forest and then follow the signs to the camping area. The first day ride is mostly uphill, but the distance travelled is modest, about 13 miles, leaving ample time to set up camp, buy dinner and go for a swim.

Monday

Monday's trip is a bit longer because it goes all around Stockbridge, but the reward is a free day Tuesday and two nights in the Red Lion Inn, perhaps the county's most famous lodging place.

Leave the Beartown State Forest via the entrance on Route 23 and head west towards Great Barrington for 2.3 miles where Monument Valley Road comes in at the right. If you go down the long hill to Great Barrington past the Butternut Basin ski area, you've gone too far. Take the Monument Valley Road, one of the nicer bicycling stretches in the county both for its views and the evenness of its grade, for 4.6 miles and its intersection with Route 7.

After pausing to admire the Monument Mountain cliff (taking advantage of a picnic area) where legend tells of an Indian maiden who leaped to her death over an unhappy love affair, go left on Route 7 downhill for nearly a mile. The ride goes right at a sign that points to "Rt. 183 — Housatonic 3." At this point you are on Ride 9, described earlier. Follow the road in from Route 7 for 0.4 miles, then go right on Route 183, pedaling 1.2 miles to the Rising Paper Mill on your left, a massive building with impressive industrial 19th century architecture, and then another 1.1 miles to the village of Housatonic.

Follow Route 183 through Housatonic, taking a right after the bridge over the river and start gradually climbing for about 4.3 miles to the intersection of Route 102. Ride 9 describes the terrain in more detail.

If you are tired and want to quit, take a right on Route

102 for 1.5 miles to the Stockbridge Chime Tower, and then a left for 0.4 flat miles to the Red Lion Inn. Total distance from Beartown is 16.8 miles.

But if you are still fresh, stay on Route 183 and head towards Lenox along the route outlined in Ride 10. This goes through Interlaken, alongside the Stockbridge Bowl, and past the main gate of Tanglewood to Lenox, a distance of 5.7 miles. Then continue to follow Ride 10, taking Route 7A south to Route 7 for 1.5 miles. Follow Route 7 south to the first left after the High Lawn Farm sign, 3.1 miles, then take West Road through two stop signs to Route 102 in South Lee, 2.7 miles. Go right on Route 102 for an easy two mile ride into Stockbridge and the Red Lion Inn. Total distance from Beartown is 29.9 miles.

Tuesday
Sleep late, have a good breakfast and spend the day in Stockbridge, ending it with a night of theater at the Berkshire Playhouse. Other offerings include Chesterwood and the Berkshire Garden Center (see Ride 12), Naumkeag, the Mission House, and the Old Corner House where paintings of the late Norman Rockwell are on exhibit.

Wednesday
The destination is the Pittsfield State Forest, a gradual uphill climb from Stockbridge. Follow Route 102 to West Stockbridge, a distance of four miles, and then Swamp Road from West Stockbridge to Pittsfield where it becomes Barker Road. After a hill coming out of West Stockbridge, the way is gradually rolling for a total of about 10 miles and its intersection with Route 20. Go right on Route 20 for 0.1 miles, left on Mirriam Street for 0.7 miles, then left on West Street to Churchill Street for 2.0 miles. Go right on Churchill Street for 1.5 miles to the Pittsfield State Forest and then go left at the sign to the state forest for another 0.7 miles. Total distance from Stockbridge is 19 miles.

Thursday
Spend a day in Pittsfield, choosing among side trips to Arrowhead, the home of Herman Melville, the Crane Museum in Dalton, the Berkshire Museum in Pittsfield, or just shop in downtown Pittsfield or swim at the municipal swimming area at Pontoosuc Lake.

To get to Park Square in Pittsfield, go back the way you

Berkshire Museum, just off Park Square in Pittsfield, is well worth the visit for anyone interested in county's history.

came, following West Street all the way to Park Square. Park Square to the Crane Museum is described in Ride 17. Park Square to Arrowhead is done by heading east on East Street to the third set of lights, 0.4 miles, then bearing right on Elm Street, following it for 0.6 miles to Holmes Road, where you go right for two miles to Arrowhead.

Friday

Friday is the big one, the first leg of the trip up and over Mount Greylock, a spectacular ride that can either end by camping out at the Stony Ledge campground or by going all the way to the summit and staying in the modest accommodations at Bascom Lodge. Mount Greylock is the state's highest peak, and the climb is long, but gradual. The views from the summit and along the way make the trip well worth the while.

The trip is described more fully in the introduction, Rides 20A and 21. As you come down off Mount Greylock to North Adams take the left on Route 2 to Williamstown.

Saturday-Sunday

Spend the night in Williamstown, either at the Williams Inn or in one of the several motels on Route 2. Try to arrive in time for a Saturday night performance at the Williamstown Summer Theatre, where a highly professional company spends its summers. You might also plan to eat at any of Williamstown's several fine restaurants, a selection of which is close enough to the center of town for easy biking. Sunday's activities should include a visit to the Sterling and Francine Clark Art Institute or biking on any one of rides 24 to 27 out of Williamstown.

Sunday-Monday

Head over to North Adams on Sunday afternoon, planning to stay either at the Sheraton Inn in the center of town, the Windsor Lake campground, which affords good swimming about a mile from town, or at the Clarksburg State Park on Route 8, about 3.5 miles north of North Adams.

Aside from swimming at Windsor Lake or the state park, North Adams offers a crafts center in the Windsor Mill where a dozen or so crafts people and artisans work under the auspices of Hoosuck Community Resources Corporation. In the planning stages at this writing are a Hoosac Tunnel Museum and an urban park reflecting the city's tex-

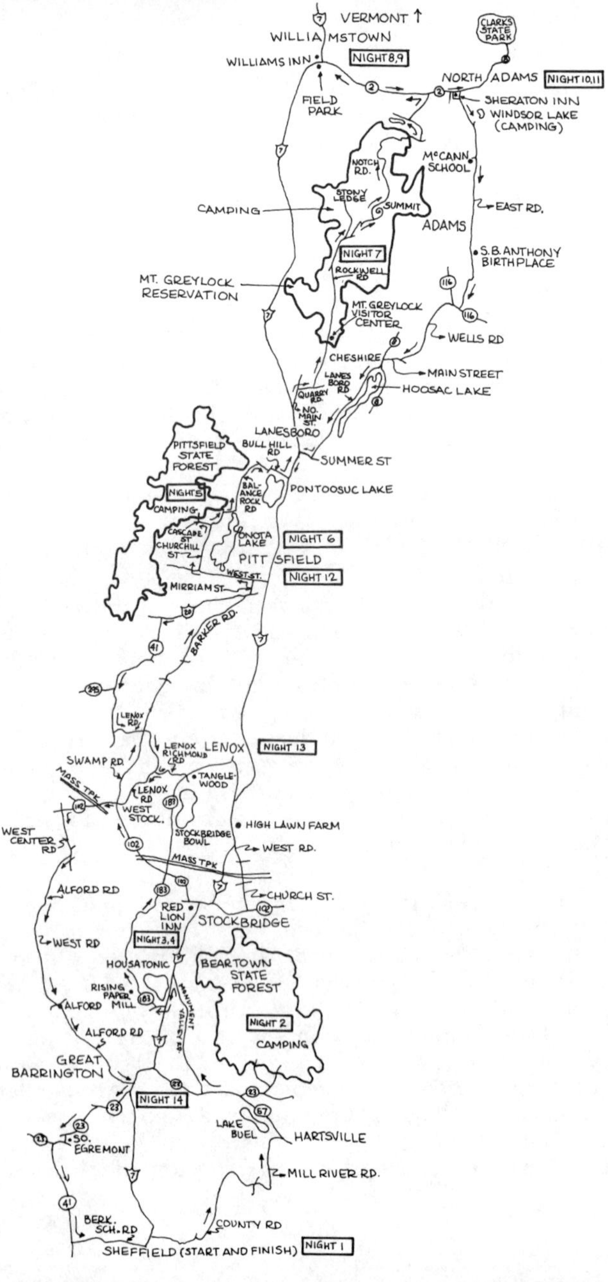

VERMONT
WILLIAMSTOWN
WILLIAMS INN
NIGHT 8,9
CLARKS STATE PARK
NORTH ADAMS
NIGHT 10,11
SHERATON INN
WINDSOR LAKE (CAMPING)
FIELD PARK
NOTCH RD.
McCANN SCHOOL
STONY LEDGE
SUMMIT
CAMPING
EAST RD.
ADAMS
NIGHT 7
S.B. ANTHONY BIRTHPLACE
ROCKWELL RD
MT. GREYLOCK RESERVATION
MT. GREYLOCK VISITOR CENTER
WELLS RD
CHESHIRE
LANES BORO RD
MAIN STREET
QUARRY RD.
HOOSAC LAKE
NO. MAIN ST.
LANESBORO
PITTSFIELD STATE FOREST
BULL HILL RD
SUMMER ST
BAL-ANCE ROCK RD
PONTOOSUC LAKE
NIGHT 5
CAMPING
CASCADE ST
CHURCHILL ST
ONOTA LAKE
NIGHT 6
PITTSFIELD
WEST ST.
NIGHT 12
MIRRIAM ST.
BARKER RD.
LENOX RD
LENOX RICHMOND RD
LENOX
NIGHT 13
SWAMP RD.
MASS TPK
TANGLEWOOD
LENOX RD
WEST STOCK.
HIGH LAWN FARM
WEST CENTER RD
STOCKBRIDGE BOWL
WEST RD.
MASS TPK
ALFORD RD
CHURCH ST.
RED LION INN
STOCKBRIDGE
WEST RD
NIGHT 3,4
HOUSATONIC
BEARTOWN STATE FOREST
RISING PAPER MILL
MONUMENT VALLEY RD
ALFORD
NIGHT 2
ALFORD RD
CAMPING
GREAT BARRINGTON
NIGHT 14
LAKE BUEL
HARTSVILLE
SO. EGREMONT
MILL RIVER RD.
BERK. SCH. RD
COUNTY RD
SHEFFIELD (START AND FINISH)
NIGHT 1

tile heritage. You might also want to visit the new campus of North Adams State College or the Natural Bridge.

Tuesday

Take Ride 20, the North-South Link, to downtown Pittsfield and plan to stay at the Hilton Inn, the Pittsfield State Forest again, or a motel. Distance is about 27 miles.

Wednesday

Plan to go to the Hancock Shaker Village by following Route 20 out of Pittsfield to the village, a distance of 4.6 miles. After spending some time at the village head south on Route 41 for 5.0 miles, going gradually downhill until Lenox Road comes in from the left. Go left on Lenox Road for 1.2 miles, cross Barker Road and then go up and over Lenox Mountain, a steep climb for 1.8 miles, then downhill to Route 183 for 1.5 miles coming out just south of the entrance to Tanglewood. Go left to Lenox for 1.6 miles, a total distance of 15.7 miles. Plan to stay in one of the many Lenox area lodging places.

Thursday

This is one of the prettier rides of the trip, but it involves a hilly start back over the Lenox Mountain, taking a left at its top and going downhill 2.2 miles to West Stockbridge.

From West Stockbridge pick up Ride 5 to Great Barrington. Head west on Route 102, going past the Old Shaker Mill, an antique place on your left, and past where Route 41 bears off to the right, going over the Massachusetts Turnpike. Take a left at West Center Road 1.9 miles from the center of town. This threads through magnificent farm scenery for 3.0 miles until the ride bears right on the Alford Road, heading south for 4.9 miles to the center of Alford. At Alford keep bearing left around the triangle in the center and head downhill for 2.6 miles to the Albert Schweitzer Center and another 1.7 miles to the intersection with Route 7 in Great Barrington. Plan to spend the night in the motel or in the Fairfield Inn on Route 23, just south of Great Barrington. Total distance is 17.3 miles.

Friday

Head back to Sheffield and the start of the two-week trip.

The trip described is leisurely and could easily be shortened to a week, with the following itinerary.

Saturday Sheffield to Stockbridge.
Sunday Stockbridge to Pittsfield State Forest.
Monday Pittsfield State Forest to summit of Mount Greylock, or Stony Ledge campground.
Tuesday Summit of Mount Greylock to Williamstown.
Wednesday Williamstown to Pittsfield.
Thursday Pittsfield to Lenox via Shaker Village.
Friday Lenox to Sheffield.

About the Author

Lewis C. Cuyler is executive editor of *The Transcript*, the daily newspaper for northern Berkshire County that is published in North Adams. An enthusiastic bicyclist and skier (cross-country and downhill), he has written extensively about both sports.

He and his wife, Harriet, their assorted bicycles and skis, live in an old house in North Adams whose needs compete for time with the beckoning trips described in this guide.